Sportbiking: "The Real World"

THE ADVANCED RIDER'S HANDBOOK

Gary S. Jaehne

Sportbiking: "The Real World"

THE ADVANCED RIDER'S HANDBOOK

Gary S. Jaehne

PUBLISHED BY:
BRENTWOOD CHRISTIAN PRESS
4000 BEALLWOOD AVENUE
COLUMBUS, GEORGIA 31904

Dedication

This book is dedicated to
The Leatherneck Racing Team
✦✦✦ **Jill and Jonathan** ✦✦✦
who have always been my
biggest fans
and supporters.

Contents

Sportbiking: "The Real World"

Supplement: Rain Riding
"The Wet Weather Rider's Guidebook"

Sportbiking:
"The Real World"

Foreword

The material and *philosophy* presented in this sportriders handbook is <u>not</u> for everybody. Prior to dedicating a great deal of time digging deeper into the meat of this publication; I recommend that you stop and ask yourself the question: "IS THIS HANDBOOK REALLY MEANT FOR ME?" Responding to the questions, posed at the conclusion of the four situations listed below, should allow you to make the proper decision. Take just a moment to read each of the questions and select the answer that most accurately reflects your probable course of action, if faced with the specified circumstances.

1: If I were riding my sportbike down a beautiful stretch of two lane mountain road (with it's lanes separated by a solid double yellow line), on clear Sunday afternoon, and came up upon a large motorhome that was traveling at 10 MPH <u>below</u> the posted 55 MPH speed limit I would ....

A) remain behind it for an indefinite period of time, until it pulled over or until a section of dotted yellow line eventually appeared (regardless of the how many miles it required) .

B) if after several opportunities for the vehicle to pull over were ignored, pass the motorhome when the oncoming traffic was clear, providing no law enforcement was readily visible.

2: Before leaving the house to begin a nice sunny 80 degree summer day of spirited sportbike riding, on my favorite twisty mountain road, I always reach for ....

A) my tank top T-shirt, Oakley® "Blades" sunglasses, baggy shorts, and Nike® hightops so I'll be comfortable and look real "cool" for the chicks at the gathering spot.

B) my helmet, gloves, leathers (jacket at least) and boots.

3: If I were traveling down a straight stretch of mountain road at about 30 MPH, and an oncoming car were to make an unannounced left hand turn directly in front of me, I would ....

A) lock up the rear brake and "lay 'er down" to avoid running straight into the car.

B) immediately scan the scene for an escape route to steer towards, to avoid the impact, while initially applying some front brake to reduce speed.

4: If I were offered a free motorcycle riding school, when I bought a new motorcycle I would ....

A) NOT go, because I already know how to ride just fine (probably better than the Instructors) and they wouldn't be able to teach me anything that I don't already know anyway.

B) take the school because there's always room for improvement in my riding skills.

If you answered "A" to any of the above questions, the chances are that this handbook is **NOT** for you! That does NOT mean that your answers were _wrong_, (as I respect the diversity of opinions and personalities that motorcycling encompasses) it simply indicates that your philosophy on issues related to motorcycling are not well suited to the majority of the subject matter that will be presented in this handbook. If you answered "**B**" to all four questions, congratulations (I guess) you appear to have the mentality, basic motorcycle knowledge and behavioral traits that make you a part of the infamous family of *"REAL WORLD"* SPORTBIKERS (curse that it might be).

The term *"REAL WORLD"*, in the title of this handbook, is intended to immediately let the potential reader know that there's something **unconventional** about the content of this handbook. The material herein, will address some aspects of sportbike riding that are normally considered as "taboo", by most motorcycle publications. Though considered "taboo" by many, they are activities that occur on a regular basis in the *"REAL WORLD"* that we ride, and therefore demand attention.

Being a part of this *"REAL WORLD"* fraternity, often brings with it the stereotyped label of *"OUTLAW"*, from the more conservative facets of our society. A simplified version of WEBSTER's definition for the word *"OUTLAW"* is: *a person who frequently commits an act that violates the law*. As bad as that definition initially sounds, it becomes a natural first reaction to deny oneself as belonging to such a fraternity. Apply this definition in the **literal** sense, however, and a very different view arises. FOR EXAMPLE: A father is driving his family down the highway to Grandma's house, for Thanksgiving dinner, maintaining a consistent 65 MPH with the main traffic flow (on a road posted at the previous national speed limit of 55 MPH). Does the word *"OUTLAW"* come to mind? I would think not; yet if held to the **absolute definition** of the word; we would have to say YES!

When more than 90% of the people are regularly violating a particular law, it should be clearly apparent (even to our most conservative elected officials) that there is something seriously wrong with the law, **not** with the people! The point I'm trying to make here is that motorcyclists certainly do not have a monopoly on being "lawbreakers", as almost everyone is an *"OUTLAW"* to some degree in their everyday life. The only variation is the degree at which we sportbikers obtain this status. The performance capabilities of todays modern sportbikes simply make us more susceptible to exceeding the boundaries of these legalities by a greater amount than "JOE AVERAGE" motorist.

8

It may seem strange at first to see any form of written material that discusses, and even instructs on riding techniques involved in, this type of *"unacceptable"* (yet regularly occuring) behavior. A behavior exhibited (in varying degrees) by millions of motorcycle riders worldwide. Many of the viewpoints presented in this handbook will be dramatically different than the *vanilla* flavored commentaries that motorcyclists are accustomed to reading in the many of the national newspapers, magazines, and "how to" handbooks (especially those published in the USA).

You'll notice that I made a special point of indicating that this approach appears primarily in publications *"published in the United States"*. The reason I made this distinction, is because I recently had the good fortune of stumbling across several excellent glossy cover European sportbike magazines (available at very select bookstores). I found the content of these publications to be extremely refreshing, as they pulled no punches in their literary style, editorial content, real-world language or actual riding photography. Though some may feel that these publications push the boundaries of good taste a little too far (and I must agree on some occasions), they do a far superior job of addressing the "grass-roots" level motorcyclist by not *"sterilizing"* or over glamourizing the sport. They help achieve this "grass-roots" result by NOT outfitting their test riders with brand new $3,000 riding gear on $15,000 motorcycles: something most of us can only dream about. I highly recommend that you seek out one of these magazines (as difficult as they are to find), to experience the taste of a very different flavor of motorcycle publication.

The "how to" books, that I mentioned before, while certainly addressing important riding techniques (from which I learned a great deal in my earlier stages of riding), always reference the racetrack environment in the bulk of their discussions, while "public road" riding (where unfortunately 90% of us do the majority of our actual sportbike riding) is portrayed in a *"knight in shining armor"* fashion. Realistically, I would project that a rider survey of all the buyers of the most famous series of "how to ride" books, would result in the following breakdown: 10%

Racers, 20% riders with at least one track day experience, and **70% riders** who have never touched a motorcycle wheel to anything but a "public road". Though I **STRONGLY** recommend that all sportbikers take the opportunity to get their bikes out onto the racetrack for a track school (i.e. DP SAFETY SCHOOL, etc...), when wanting to test the full capabilities of themselves and their bike; I recognize that it's impractical to expect a "real world" sportbiker to totally curtail any other form of spirited riding during, the other 360 + days of the year. Those other 360 + days of riding, is the world I will be addressing in this publication.

I have been riding motorcycles on the street for over 13 years, raced MOTO-X (in the dirt) for 8 years and have been roadracing at the club and limited national level (WERA, AMA), for the last 6 years. During that period of time I have regularly subscribed to numerous motorcycle publications and it has always bothered me, especially of late, that these publications can often be very hypocritical in their portrayal of the modern day sportbike rider. What do I mean by that? Example: on the cover of most current sportbike oriented magazines you will see a picture showing one or more of the magazine test riders dragging their knees through a high speed corner, on a **public** road (as witnessed by the clearly visible double-yellow line in the background), while in the same issue you will find an editorial article stressing the importance of safety and law abidance in the street riding environment. There is invariably a disclaimer statement, inside the cover, stating the these shots were taken on a stretch of road that had been closed for special photographic use, but the implied message to the subscriber remains. I understand that the primary reason for these magazines outward conservatism and "holier than thou" approach, is the liability concerns that would arise from a large publication condoning any form of *"real world"* behavior. The staff and writers for these publications certainly know that the majority of their dedicated subscribers participate in some level of *"REAL WORLD"* SPORTBIKE riding on a regular basis. The pictures they display showing their riders behaving in this fashion, serves to sell magazines, as well as to stimulate rider's desire to buy the latest sportbike offerings from the manufacturers (in an attempt to emulate their heroes). It's ridiculous to think that a true sportbike enthusiast will see their model of motorcycle portrayed in this exuberant riding fashion, within these publications, and then be content with a leisurely "putt" down the local canyons at the 45 MPH posted speed limit, while following a fully loaded motorhome.

An outstanding example of the contradictions between what is technically "legal" and what is practiced in the "real world", was shown to me on a recent sunny Sunday morning sportbike ride.

* * * *

ACTUAL RIDING EXPERIENCE:

This ride would not have been anything unusual except for the fact that an additional rider had been added to our normal group; an off-duty Highway Patrol Officer (and avid motorcycle enthusiast). I started the ride leading the group, with our extra rider following directly behind me. I felt very apprehensive about my riding, as I set the pace for the group, first keeping the speed near the posted limit then gradually stepping it up while closely viewing our #2 rider, in my mirrors, for his reactions. He maintained his distance throughout all gradual increases in pace so I began to be more bold in my riding as we settled into "THE PACE". The final measuring stick, for his behavior, occurred as we encountered slow traffic (on this two lane, double yellow lined road) and I needed to make a decision on whether to pass or remain behind. Our special #2 rider closed the distance behind me, indicating his expectations of an eminent pass, so I checked for clear traffic and made the move with him following closely in my draft. This final move established the "rules of the day", and the remaining part of our ride went on uneventfully, at our normal sportbike "PACE". The irony of this whole situation was the fact that the next day, this same individual would be writing traffic tickets for vehicles violating many of the laws he had regularly broken on our ride.

* * * *

Now don't get me wrong, I'm 100% in favor of safety, as that's my primary objective in writing this handbook. That safety philosophy does not, however, necessarily mean <u>absolute</u> adherence to all traffic laws, especially under impractical conditions. This non-adherence applies particularly to laws related to overly conservative speed limits (realistic only for behemoth sized motorhomes pulling trailers) on wide spacious roads in unpopulated areas AND excessive use of <u>endless</u> double yellow lines, on 10 mile continuous stretches of road. In many cases, less than 10 years ago, these same roads were considered perfectly safe with the opposing traffic separated by nothing more than a single BROKEN yellow line. The overall road conditions or driver/rider visibility available on these roads did not change, to necessitate the replacement of these dotted lines with the governmentally imposed double yellow "wall"; only a bureaucratic decision made in the name of "safety", brought about these apparently permanent changes. Most of the more advanced sportriding techniques described in this handbook **DO NOT** apply to riding done on heavily populated city streets or highly traveled freeways/highways. These are areas where general restraint and DEFENSIVE riding techniques, <u>not</u> speed oriented riding techniques, should be applied! *(Enough preaching from me; right?)*

So you may ask the question why would anyone want to write a handbook admitting to, and even instructing in techniques on this form of *"REAL WORLD"* riding? The answer is simple. If we censored all mention of this form of riding from all publications in the world, this very minute, and stressed absolute safety and law abidance exhaustively throughout, would it result in all the sportbike riders either selling their prized possession, or riding them in such a conservative manner that absolutely no traffic laws were ever violated? *(The answer to that question is quite obvious)*

I learned long ago in life an important fact (one that ostriches are stereotyped as regularly ignoring: i.e. "head buried in the sand"); that **DENYING** the existence of something undesirable (that <u>is</u> real and <u>does</u> exist) will definitely <u>NOT</u> make it go away. The existence of *"REAL WORLD"* SPORTBIKE riding in America, and the rest of the world, is and will continue to be <u>real</u> as long as there are sportbikes available, people to ride

12

them, and open roads to beckon their performance. As this form of riding cannot realistically be eliminated, it makes sense to pull our heads out of the sand (ostrich analogy again) and discuss it openly, so that we might find a way to help make participation in this activity less of a risk to the riders while also chasing away the black cloud that often hovers over the public image of the motorcycling community.

My desire to write this handbook has been brought to a fever pitch by the number of tragic deaths, and serious injuries that have occurred at my local sportbike riding area during the last two years. Many of those deaths and injuries have, unfortunately, involved reasonably close friends. As sad as each of these occurrences have been, the most depressing part for me has been that in every single one of these accidents the rider(s) violated one or more of the primary rules for the *"REAL WORLD"* SPORTBIKE rider (rules that will be discussed during the course of this handbook). Though automobiles were partially at fault, in most of these incidents, the riders could have avoided the final outcome through the religious application of <u>ALL</u> of these rules.

I consider myself to be a very *"LUCKY"* motorcycle rider. Lucky in the respect that during my many years of riding and racing I have experienced a tremendous number of "close calls"; "close calls" that I can sit here and still be able to write about today. The majority of the rules discussed in this handbook, were learning discoveries that were born from one or more of these "close calls". Each time I experienced one of these incidents I would immediately (once I caught my breath) analyze the situation to answer three major questions:

1: Did I do anything wrong that created this situation?

2: What things did I do right that allowed me to survive?

3: What technique can I apply in my future riding to reduce the risk of a reoccurrence?

Each time I answered these questions the knowledge gained was immediately deposited into my riding skills "account",

13

increasing the reserves, in preparation for my inevitable next withdrawal (next "close call"). The problem lies with the fact that, unfortunately, not all sportbike riders are *"LUCKY"* riders (though I honestly hope that you are). These riders cannot afford to allow themselves to gradually learn, over many years, from their mistakes. Their riding skill accounts will be called upon for an enormous withdrawal, early on in their riding experiences, and therefore those individuals **must** find an accelerated method of acquiring this knowledge, from some other source. Providing a "SOURCE" for that form of accelerated learning, is my primary objective in writing this handbook. It's kind of like encapsulating twenty years of motorcycle learning into a pill that, once swallowed (or read in this case), may help protect a rider against the dangers that await him in the real world of motorcycle riding. QUESTION: What makes me think that these techniques are effective in actual practice? ANSWER: I have put in over 100,000 miles of sportbike riding, exclusively on twisty mountain backroads, in just the last six years. The cornering forces obtained, during most of those rides, were consistently exhilarating. The riding was done under all conditions (rain, cold, darkness, etc..) and during that entire time I am pleased to report of only a single actual accident, that occurred in the rain on spilled diesel fuel, with minor damage to the bike and NO injuries to myself. That 100,000 mile window of riding included many "challenging" occurrences that put these techniques to the ultimate test. Looking back on that record, I present to you, with absolute confidence, that these techniques are sound and will serve to benefit the sportbike rider. If only a single *"UNLUCKY"* sportbike rider (who has read this handbook) encounters only a single occurrence that he can look back on as a "close call", knowing that a technique described herein helped save him; I will have been successful.

Chapter 1

Basic Philosophy

In reading and answering the questions, on the first page of this handbook, you had a sneak preview of this philosophy. Now let's take a deeper look into the mind of the *"REAL WORLD"* SPORT-BIKE RIDER. The *"REAL WORLD"* SPORTBIKE RIDER ...

- searches for roads to ride that have the following characteristics:

  - ► low degree of automobile traffic
  - ► few (to no) cross-streets, intersections, driveways
  - ► maximum # of turns per mile (tighter turns are better)
  - ► few long straightaways (discourages top speed runs)
  - ► minimal (to no) double yellow lines (if possible)
  - ► low degree of law enforcement
  - ► good road surface condition
  - ► familiarity with the road and it's obstacles

- utilizes his bikes performance where it counts; <u>in the corners</u>

- maintains reasonable speeds in straightaways, as he views them as nothing more than <u>necessary</u> links between sets of corners

- treats the yellow line, in the middle of a corner, as a **<u>WALL</u>** (unless passing)

- establishes a "pecking order" within his group of riders and respects that order during all rides

- knows his own skill level and rides within himself (is <u>realistic</u> about his ability)

- wears all the protective equipment possible, always dressing for "the crash" not just "for the ride"

- checks and maintains his bike's proper condition, to insure it's maximum level of performance (which conveniently improves his safety as well)

- recognizes the risks of his sport, and **accepts** them.

- possesses a deep love of motorcycling that will last a lifetime

These represent the basic guidelines that allow the sportbike rider to be able obtain the maximum satisfaction from his riding while minimizing the risks.

I'm sure everyone has ridden with some guy that has a high powered bike and insists on accelerating to maximum speed in all straightaways, only to "park the thing" when he enters the next set of corners. Certainly it's his bike and his decision as to the way he wishes to ride, but this behavior is not tolerated within the *"REAL WORLD"* SPORTBIKERS philosophy and therefore this rider should be required to change his ways or seek other riding partners.

I've seen more of these type of riders over the years, than I would like, and in too many cases these rider's sportbike riding days are brought to an untimely halt, in the most unfortunate of ways. In my attempts to analyze what evokes these riding traits, the most common cause seems to be nothing more than a lack of riding skill and experience. There certainly is a large amount of "EGO" involved in riding sportbikes. I believe that most male sportbike riders still view going fast on a motorcycle as a "macho" thing to be able to do (I must admit that I still have a bit of that attitude creeping around in my bones, as well). A rider who purchases his first sportbike often feels pressure to perform at a level befitting of the image that the bike itself portrays. I mean "hey if Scott Russell can do certain things on basically the same bike, I should be able to too." This new rider definitely does not possess the ability to go through the corners at the speed potential of a modern sportbike (corners are the true measuring stick of a riders skill level). The new rider will often attempt to mask (and even deny to himself) this inadequacy by twisting the throttle wide open in every straightaway (where absolutely NO riding skill is required) to compensate. This wide-open approach to straightaway speed, inevitably leads to overcharging of the corners and eminent disaster.

* * * *

ACTUAL RIDING EXPERIENCE:

How do I know what thoughts can go through the mind of a rider exhibiting this type of behavior? I am almost embarrassed to admit it, but I can recall one experience (just after reentering the sportbike arena in 1989, riding a brand new, just introduced, shiny green Kawasaki ZX-7) where I met up with a talented group of riders. Several of the riders were on smaller displacement bikes (i.e. TZR-250, RGV-250 two-strokes). I found my "EGO" badly showing, as they passed me on a stretch of mountain road, and found myself immediately holding the throttle wide open until I passed most of them back in the next long straightaway. Approaching the next set of corners at well over 120 MPH, I panicked and hit the front and rear brakes, causing the rear tire to skid and hop, in a crude attempt to regain control. Fortunately I did NOT crash the bike (that's one of the "close call" experiences that I was "LUCKY" enough to have survived to learn from), but the other riders did repass me, and thinking back on it now, I can imagine the thoughts going through their heads ("what a squid!"). The only positive thing I can say, in my own defense, is that at least I was wearing full leathers, boots, helmet, and gloves. Still a pretty stupid move though, huh?

* * * *

The long term application of this type of riding style is a sure invitation to disaster, as one of two possible scenarios will likely occur:

A: The rider will encounter another vehicle crossing his path (i.e. left turn, car pulling out from a side road, etc..)

while at this warp speed, and be unable to react in time to avoid the impact.

B: The rider, not having refined his ability to sense actual speed, will enter the next corner (at the end of the straightaway) at such an extreme speed that he will panic, likely applying excessive brakes while entering the corner, and cross over the yellow line into whatever fate awaits him.

Obviously neither of this scenarios have a very happy ending for the rider or for the sport of motorcycle riding.

* * * *

ACTUAL RIDING EXPERIENCE:

One Sunday afternoon at our usual gathering spot, we started our bikes up in preparation of heading off onto a fantastic stretch of roads that we refer to as "THE LOOP". The group consisted of about twelve riders (a large number by our typical standards) and excitement was high in expectation of a great ride. One of the riders there that day, that had only recently attached himself to our group on selected occasions, was riding a Kawasaki ZX-7. His riding gear consisted of a "bomber type" leather jacket, helmet, gloves and jeans. The first time I ever met him, he was boldly boasting about how he and his other friends (both with ZX-7's) were the fastest guys on the road and that no one had ever "beaten" them. The first couple of rides he did with our group were somewhat of a humbling experience for him, as he found that many other riders were able to exceed his riding skills (in the corners). After a couple of rides, it seemed as though he had learned some good lessons, and deflated his ego down to a safe level. On this day, however, his ego must have been recharged to full capacity again. As we started the ride, on this day, I was leading our group through the twisty backroads that make this particular ride such an enjoyable experience. I didn't pay particular attention to which rider, of the group, was next in line behind me (as I always maintain my primary atten-

18

tion on what lies ahead of me). Entering a right hand corner, on a especially tight section of road, I noticed a green front wheel to my left. Surprised, I maintained my focus on the road ahead in preparation for the next set of corners. Down the next short straightaway I was again surprised as the green ZX-7 roared past, with our newcomer pilot aboard. (NOTE: The street bike I was riding at the time was a moderately powered, but nimble, 400cc sport-standard model called a Honda CB-1). Approaching the next corner, I decided it was safer to follow him than to attempt a pass to reestablish the previous riding order. This also offered me an opportunity to observe his riding style to see if he had truly improved to this new level of performance. Following him briefly, I saw that he was taking very poor lines entering the corners and riding rather erratically. I passed him back, on the brakes, as he was holding up the pace and I didn't really feel safe being riding behind him. Simplifying the remaining hour of the ride; he continually overshot corners (almost running into the side of the mountain on several occasions), and ran across dou-ble-yellow lines (into the opposing lane), all in an attempt to "beat everybody". He was warned repeatedly by numerous rid-ers, at regrouping stops, that his riding was extremely ragged, putting himself and others in jeopardy of serious injury. Miraculously he escaped any injury on that day. Less than one month later, however, he was involved in a serious accident in which he entered a corner at excessive speed then proceeded to lock up his rear brake, mid-turn, crashing and causing the rider following him to go down. Fortunately both riders survived, though moderately injured, to ride another day.

* * * *

Chapter 2

Preparing to Ride

On a clear and warm Sunday afternoon, a stroll through the parking lot of our local sportriding rendezvous spot, will unveil an incredibly diverse mix of people. This mix includes such variables as height, weight, age, sex, occupation, financial status, riding experience, etc.... As a result of the influence of one or more of these variables, you will see just as diverse a selection of brands and types of motorcycles. Closer observation will show that this variety continues on to one more level: that of **riding apparel**.

For the novice rider; seeing this wide array of variations that are obviously selected by the experienced motorcycle riding fraternity, might leave them scratching their head, while inquisitively thinking: "what is **the** _PROPER_ riding equipment that a sportbike rider should use"?

One of the most enticing aspects of motorcycling, is the freedom that it offers it's participants. This freedom extends itself into the process of selecting what type of riding gear will be used by each motorcyclist. One of these freedoms (selection of whether or not to wear a helmet) has recently been removed by the local governments, in many states. Despite the government mandate that all riders must wear <u>A HELMET</u>, the variety in the types, styles, brands, and colors that are selected, shows that the free spirit of the motorcyclist is not easily suppressed.

As I too respect this freedom, I'm not going to get into any extended lectures telling you what equipment you **MUST** wear. Instead, I will merely leave you with a list of the type of protective apparel that I **RECOMMEND**. This recommendation is based upon my own personal experiences with injury occurrence/avoidance that have resulted from "get-offs", while in various states of protective attire. I guess you could say some of these lessons were learned from the infamous "SCHOOL OF HARD KNOCKS".

RECOMMENDED SPORTRIDING EQUIPMENT:

PRIMARY GEAR:

- **FULL COVERAGE HELMET:** (DOT/Snell approved, properly sized to the riders head, no previous shock damage: *never crashed*)
- **LEATHER GLOVES:** (good quality of adequate thickness, extending well over the wrist and reinforced in the palm area: i.e. rivets, Kevlar, etc..)
- **LEATHER BOOTS:** (good quality, extending well above the ankle; plastic skid protection in the ankle area are a plus)
- **LEATHER JACKET/PANTS/ or FULL SUIT:** (good quality of adequate thickness, with padded armor in shoulders, elbow/forearm, hips, and knee/shin areas. Built in back protection is a real plus)

EXTRA PROTECTION:

- **BACK PROTECTOR:** (strap on type, with hard plastic plates along entire spine area)
- **SUN GLASSES:** (weather/time of day permitting)
- **ANTI-FOG SHIELD/APPLICANT:** (weather dependent)

Acquiring the entire list of the above items can be a rather substantial *investment*. I like the word *investment*, because I firmly believe that outfitting yourself with first rate protective equipment, is truly an *investment* in your future health. Kind of like buying medical insurance: you buy it, but hope you never really need to use it.

Purchased <u>new</u>, it's reasonable to expect to spend a total cost of **$750,** to as much as **$2,500.** Obviously your own personal financial situation will have a major impact on your selection of these items. Used riding equipment is often advertised, at very reasonable prices, in the classified section of many nationally distributed motorcycle newspapers. These publications are a good potential source for leathers, boots, and gloves, but I wouldn't recommend buying a used helmet; your head is too important.

Over the years, I've come across a few motorcyclists at our local gathering spot, on brand new (and extremely high powered) sportbikes, decked out in nothing more than a helmet (as required by our current law). Some of these riders weren't even wearing <u>gloves</u>. While engaging in conversation with one individual, I casually inquired into the reasoning behind his rather limited riding attire. He responded by saying that the purchase of his shiny new toy had consumed all his resources, leaving him without enough money left over to buy any riding gear.

His answer, though it seemed legitimate enough, made me begin thinking to myself, "was there any other option that he could have used?". Pondering the idea for a bit, an idea came to mind. Assuming this sportrider had financed the bike (as most new motorcycle purchases are these days), the additional cost of leathers, boots, gloves, etc... (most likely available through the same dealer) could have been added-on to the total amount borrowed during the initial purchase. This would have allowed him to defray the total cost of the riding apparel over the same two-three year financing period of the existing loan. The increase in his monthly payment would have been minimal.

I'll end this topic with an old adage that I didn't invent, but firmly believe.

•••• **DRESS FOR THE CRASH, NOT FOR THE RIDE!** ••••

Chapter 3

General Techniques

ALWAYS RIDE TO THE RIGHT OR LEFT OF CENTER OF YOUR LANE

The center portion of the lane is the area occupied by the "drip zone" of all the automobiles that have preceded you down the road. That portion of those vehicles is where all the leaking radiators, loose oil drain plugs, and seeping transmissions drop their residues. Minimizing the amount of time you spend in the center of your lane will decrease your chances of an unwelcome surprise.

Other debris (rocks, nails, sticks, etc..) that may have found it's way onto the road, is also most likely to be encountered in the center of the lane because the tires from automobiles will continuously track through two strips to the left and right of center, acting like vacuum cleaners, picking up and discarding (off the road or in the center) items that may initially find their way onto those two portions of the road. Motorcyclists experiencing more flat tires than the norm, may likely be guilty of regularly riding around the center of the lane. In wet weather riding, utilizing these areas will again benefit the motorcyclist, due to the displacement of the standing water, as a result of the spinning car tires.

LATE APEX ALL CORNERS (ESPECIALLY LEFT HAND TURNS)

I know that most "how to ride" books use the term "APEX" fluently, assuming that all their readers fully understand it's meaning. Well for those of you who are not racetrack oriented, let me give a quick definition:

23

APEX: During the execution of a turn, the single point at which the motorcycle is at the absolute **innermost** position in the lane.

Late apexing, means continuing straight into the corner as far as is safely possible, before initiating the actual turning maneuver (counter-steering). Late apexing is one of those magical riding techniques that serves two contrasting, yet both very useful, purposes. First, this technique is typically the **FASTEST** method of executing most corners, by providing the straightest possible exit line out. The second benefit is that it improves your **SAFETY** margin by allowing for the widest angle of view, through the corner, before committing yourself to the turn. This can help prevent a head-on impact with an oncoming vehicle (while you are executing a left-hand turn) that has lazily decided to drift over and use up two or three feet of your lane.

* * * *

ACTUAL RIDING EXPERIENCE:

One Sunday, we were finishing the last portion of one of our favorite short riding loops. The two lane road is a steady uphill climb, with an incredible string of interconnecting, and mildly banked corners. The turns are tight enough to insure that the average speed is maintained in the 40-60 MPH range. The right side of the road is cut closely up against the side of a small mountain, with it's face being quite vertical. I approached one of the particularly tight, "decreasing radius" right-hand corners rolling the throttle smoothly on as my eyes searched hungrily for the exit of the corner. As I steered the bike toward a planned late apex, into this relatively blind corner, I was shocked to suddenly have two bicyclists appear. They were in the right-hand two feet of my lane, against the mountain, and were unconsciously weaving as they attempted to make the steep uphill climb. Thanks to my deep entry into the corner, and late planned apex, I was able to spot the riders just soon enough to abort my apex, initiate a reverse counter-steering maneuver and narrowly miss the bicyclists.

* * * *

RIDE ALL RIGHT HAND TURNS AT A LEVEL
NO GREATER THAN 90% OF LEFT HANDERS

The motive behind this behavior may not, at first, be obvious. Is is due to the fact that more motorcyclists are left handed than right handed? <u>No</u>; besides that statement isn't even true. Could it be because most racetracks are run in a primarily counterclockwise direction? <u>No</u>, that's not really true either.

The primary reason behind this approach, especially during faster paced riding, is <u>SURVIVAL</u>. The two scenarios, I've provided below will shed some light on this rationale:

SCENARIO #1 (Left hand turn):

The rider approaches a smooth 50 MPH **lefthand** corner, on a familiar stretch of two lane mountain road. The corner is a constant radius turn, allowing for a nice steady throttle roll-on, right out to the exit. On the outer righthand edge of the road, beyond the edge of the asphalt, is a wide flat dirt shoulder on which cars can pull out to allow for passing.

Setting up his initial entry from the far right hand side of the right lane (the ideal line to "straighten out" this corner), the rider has an excellent degree of visibility through the first half of the turn (insured of no oncoming traffic, or unexpected obstacles in his lane).

Snapping off a quick countersteering maneuver, the rider drops the bike smoothly into the entrance of the corner, with total confidence. Two-thirds of the way through, the bike encounters a small patch of loose sand, previously deposited by an overloaded pickup truck. Passing over the patch, the bike's front tire begins to slip away, causing the rider to unavoidably drift wide of his intended line, by <u>over three feet</u>. This action puts the bike only inches from the righthand edge of the pavement, where the tire (past the sandy patch) finally catches it's grip, allowing the redeemed rider to continue on down the road, shaken but uninjured!

Had the rider not had the good fortune to have gained control, before reaching the edge of the asphalt, his fate would have probably been a 40 MPH lowside across the dirt shoulder, causing repairable damage to his bike and minor (if any) injuries to himself (provided he was outfitted in full protective equipment).

SCENARIO #2 (Right hand turn):

The same rider approaches a smooth 50 MPH __righthand__ corner possessing similar characteristics to our previous example. Due to the small hillsides, that decorate the perimeter of the road, visibility is limited to about one-third of the way through the corner.

The rider drops the bike firmly into the turn with <u>confidence</u> (though in this case, due to lack of adequate visibility, not enough information was actually available to justify it). Crossing through the apex of the turn, and beginning his exit; a patch of sand is again encountered, causing the bike to begin to drift (<u>over three feet</u>) past the leftmost limits of the intended path. Unfortunately, three feet to the <u>LEFT</u> of the intended path, puts the bike over two feet <u>into the oncoming lane of traffic</u>!!

<u>Regardless</u> of whether the rider saves the actual lowside or not; <u>in this situation</u> his fate is no longer in his hands. The most skilful "save", of the initial lowside predicament, will be of little consequence, if a large truck just happens to coming up the road in the opposite direction!!

* * * *

ACTUAL RIDING EXPERIENCE:

Putting in as many serious sportriding miles as I have (40,000 +), during the last four years; I have replaced an incredible number of sets of tires. I typically get about 2,000 to 2,500 miles, maximum, out of a soft set of radial sport compound tires; resulting in at least 18 trips to the local motorcycle shop.

Each time I would remove the wheels from my bike, and load them up for transport, I would consistently make the same interesting discovery about the condition of the tires.

1) *The rear tire was always worn out more than the front, through both were previously replaced at the same time.*

2) *The <u>lefthand</u> side of both tires were worn approximately <u>15-20% more</u> than the righthand side.*

Brainstorming, in an attempt to explain this phenomenon, I determined that one major cause of the predominant wear on the rear tire (versus the front) was due to the proper application of the throttle roll-on rule, being religiously applied on my little 400cc Honda CB-1.

The second condition, of tires worn more on the left side than on the right, can be attributed to the "90% maximum" attack mentality that I apply to my righthand corners. It's not just textbook concepts; for me it's a way of __LIFE__. (Note: the "crown shape" of most roads, for water drainage< is most likely a contributing factor to this tire wear, as well)

* * * *

LOOK AS FAR AHEAD AS POSSIBLE

Maintaining the focal point for your vision as far down the road as possible, will provide you with three very important benefits:

The first benefit falls into the category of **SAFETY**. In many emergency maneuvers, the difference between being able to successfully <u>avoid</u> an impact and a devastating accident, can be nothing more than a few <u>milliseconds</u>. At 60 MPH, for each additional 100 feet that you look down the road, you will increase the amount of available reaction time (that you have to avoid a potential accident) by approximately **20** milliseconds. That 20 milliseconds can frequently be more that enough time to make all the difference.

The second advantage, that this extended vision will provide, pertains to your **SPEED** potential. The maximum speed that riders often feel safe going through a corner, is directly tied to their level of "speed sensation". In other words, the level of speed that the rider detects as he enters a corner, is based solely upon the sensory inputs he is receiving (the eyes being this primary sensory tool). The rider's detected speed is only as accurate as the source for this sensory information. If the riders focal spot is too close in front of him, that speed information will be greatly accelerated from his actual speed, often causing him to unnecessarily panic and grab a handful of brake. To prove this speed sensing effect to yourself; while riding down a straight stretch of road (with no traffic or intersections around), at a reasonable 40 MPH, look directly down at the ground below the motorcycle. Maintain that view long enough for the speed sensing circuits in your brain to process the information. Did it feel like you were traveling significantly faster than the actual 40 MPH? Now slowly and gradually shift your focal point up the road (in small intervals) until you are looking as far ahead as possible. Did you feel your speed sensation gradually diminish as you moved the focal point forwards? Can you imagine how difficult it would be to overcome the fear that would accompany traveling at over 100 MPH on a motorcycle, **if** the normal speed sensation were like the one you get when looking directly down at the moving ground.

The final improvement, that this extended vision technique will bring to your riding, occurs when riding on twisty roads with multiple interconnecting corners (lefts and rights). Inexperienced riders often make the mistake, on this type of terrain, by charging hard into the <u>first</u> sweeping left-hander, only to find that it connects directly to a tight decreasing radius right-hander. The result is a big handful of brakes (mid corner) and a probable trip over the double yellow line, as the bike tries to stands up. If the rider had moved his focal point further ahead, he would have been able to recognize the upcoming turn's tight radius, while he was still entering the first left-hander, allowing him to correctly adjust his speed for the exit.

The proper technique, for riding any road with lots of contiguous (adjoining) corners, is the same strategy used in playing a winning game of CHESS. Thinking as far ahead, as possible. In Chess, selection of each individual move is based LESS on the **current** board status, and MORE upon what effect that move will have on the **upcoming** ones. In sportriding, <u>looking</u> ahead allows for <u>thinking</u> ahead. This enables a rider to determine the optimum speed to execute a specific corner, based upon what effect it will have on the upcoming **combination** of turns. The rider must then establish a plan that will allow him to maintain the best <u>AVERAGE</u> speed through the entire section. Kenny

Roberts made a comment, years ago, that summarizes this technique in a nutshell. Simply put, his statement was: ***"Know when to go SLOW, to go FAST"***.

MAINTAIN A "WIDE SCREEN" VIEW OF THE RIDING ENVIRONMENT

Due to my defensive riding philosophy, I always view the riding environment as a potentially "hostile territory". I think of myself as the bullseye in the center of a target, with everything around me (for 360 degrees) like bullets. I've found that by always anticipating something may happen, I'm the most prepared for the moment when it eventually does (and believe me, it will). Obstacles can enter your riding path from any direction, as many unfortunate riders have discovered. Widening your "field of view" to the maximum angle, is the best single defense that you can use to protect yourself against this danger. The width of the area from which your eyes are able to obtain useable information, is much larger than you might expect. Though the level of detail that can be obtained from objects decreases proportionally with their distance from the center of your field of view, sufficient information is still available from periphery objects to allow for their detection . Knowing whether it's a Blazer or a Bronco, that's about to pull out from a side road in front of you, is of little importance. The fact that it is there is the only thing that is important to you, at that moment.

The ability to subconsciously receive **useful** information from your extreme periphery, after you develop this technique, is quite amazing.

* * * *

ACTUAL RIDING EXPERIENCE:

Over my many years of driving performance cars and motorcycles, on the street, I have become very observant of the whereabouts of law enforcement while riding: I had left my house, early one Sunday morning, traveling across what seemed like an *endless stretch of city streets (with their repetitive stop signs and red lights), on my way to the starting point for the <u>real</u> "riding" portion of our weekend sportbike ride. As I was riding conservatively, my conscious focal point was directly in front of me, paying <u>what I felt</u> was very little attention to the things occurring outside this narrow window I had created. As I continued down this rather monotonous stretch of four lane boulevard, my mind was already ten miles ahead, filled with visions of sweeping black asphalt roadways disappearing into the cool green background of the mountain's trees. Suddenly my attention was inexplicably snapped back to the present, as if I had been tapped on the shoulder by a mysterious passenger. The thought passing through my mind was "I better check my speed, I feel like there might be a Cop around". I checked by speed briefly, then scanned around me to see if there was any valid reason for this sudden concern. To my surprise, going in the opposite direction, was a black and white police car that had already passed me several several seconds before. It became quite obvious that my eyes and brain had been subconsciously (out of instilled habits of using the "wide screen view" technique) scanning to the far edges of my field of view. The fact that I was able to not only see the vehicle, but was also able to distinguish it as a police car, proved the level of detail available, even at the edges of this window. are quite adequate.*

* * * *

MAINTAIN A RAPID EYE SCAN OF THE ENTIRE RIDING SCENE

Despite the fact that the wide screen view allows a large visual sampling window, there are still areas that are not adequately analyzed within a single "snapshot". This problem is similar to that of trying to take a complete team portrait of the entire staff of the San Francisco 49ers, using a conventional camera lens. The solution to the riding problem is as simple as the solution to the photo problem, take several "snapshots", moving the sampling window prior to taking each one, to get the WHOLE picture. Each time the rider's scanning window is moved, objects that were previously located at the outer edges of the last scan (where detailed information about them was less available) will have been moved to a portion where they can be more closely interrogated.

* * * *

ACTUAL RIDING EXPERIENCE:

In my attempts to improve my riding skills; several years ago I purchased the video tape (made by Keith Code) called "TWIST OF THE WRIST". This video offered many good lessons to be learned, however after watching the tape numerous times, I noticed a subtle lesson (pertaining to the "rapid scan" technique) that the maker's of the tape had inadvertently provided the attentive viewer. The motorcycle used in the video was equipped with a "bike-cam" that allowed filming of the actual rider during laps around the Willow Springs racetrack in California. The camera was positioned such that not only the riders body motions were visible, but if you looked very closely (which I finally did after numerous viewings of the tape), the activity of the rider's __EYES__ could also be analyzed. During one track session, the eyes of the rider (a professional roadracer) could be seen rapidly scanning from left to right, __repeatedly__, during the execution of a single sweeping corner. Prior to noticing this in the video, I had never __consciously__ thought about this technique being part of my riding. Making it something that I now __consciously__ do, as part of my riding, has made me a safer rider on the street.

* * * *

MAINTAIN STEADY (BUT GRADUAL) THROTTLE ROLL-ON THROUGH THE ENTIRE CORNER

The importance of this technique stems from the desire to optimize the bike's handling by maintaining a steady 60/40 (60% Rear / 40% Front) weight distribution on the motorcycle, at all times while cornering. This last statement may bring the following question to your mind; "why would I want to place a larger percentage of the bike's weight on the rear tire, wouldn't a 50/50 balance be optimum?" A quick visual inspection of the tires on your modern day sportbike will reveal a significant difference in size between the front and rear tires. The rear tire possesses a footprint that is typically 25-40% larger than the front. That means that the rear tire has a much greater capability to endure side-loading forces that will be placed upon the motorcycle as it traverses through the corner. The <u>total</u> amount of side force placed upon the bike is determined by several factors: 1) The overall weight of the motorcycle and rider, 2) The speed at which the bike is entering the corner, 3) The turning radius demanded by the corner. The rider has very little control over this <u>total</u> amount of force (other than slowing down his pace), but a **<u>GREAT</u>** deal of control on <u>how</u> that force will be distributed to the bike's chassis.

In stock car racing, the mechanics have the ability to relocate moveable weights, within the chassis, to optimize the car's load distribution and handling characteristics for each track. The motorcycle rider has the ability to perform this same type of weight relocation, however it can be accomplished dynamically (on demand) by a simple twist of the right wrist. Amazingly, the motorcycle rider can easily transfer more than 200 pounds of weight from the front tire's load to the rear, with less than one-sixteenth of an inch of wrist rotation. The need to transfer some of this weight off of the front tire is brought about by the following fact. As the motorcycle is leaned into a high speed corner, the side forces placed upon the chassis will cause a loss of forward momentum (speed). This loss of speed is in effect deceleration, and we all know that during normal deceleration (braking) weight is automatically transferred onto the front end of the bike. If the bike is rapidly pitched into the corner, with the the throttle in the off position (wrong thing to do!), this same type of sudden weight transfer to the front will occur, resulting in exceeding the limit of the smaller front tire's grip and inevitably a bad front end slide (maybe a crash). In the same situation, if the throttle is smoothly applied immediately upon the bike being leaned into the corner, the resultant weight transfer to the rear, will compensate for the cornering forces deceleration effect (loading up of the front tire), thereby maintaining the ideal 60/40 balance throughout the turn. This keeps the side-force requirements, placed upon the front tire, well within it's load capabilities.

$$* \ * \ * \ *$$

ACTUAL RIDING EXPERIENCE:

It was my first year of roadracing, and I had become fairly comfortable on my FZR-400. The season was more than halfway over, having provided me with a considerable number of laps around my local racetrack (Sears Point). My racing performance had been good (for a novice), but like any respectable racer, I was looking for ways to improve my lap times.

I had read many books on racing techniques and found that they all agreed on one point: "the largest possible improvement in your lap times will be gained by increasing your speed through the fastest corners on the racetrack". Taking this information to heart, I decided that the highest speed corner on the track, where I could use some improvement, was the 100 MPH + right hander: turn 10. My normal technique for this corner was to approach it from the leftmost edge of the racetrack in sixth gear, click off a single downshift, perform as late of an entry as my testicle size would allow, and lastly apply a smooth application of throttle to maintain the bike's 60/40 weight balance through the corner.

In my attempt to increase my cornering speed, through this 100 MPH right hander, I modified my technique, just slightly, with some rather heart-stopping results! My initial speed in approaching the corner was about the same as before, but I had decided <u>NOT</u> to make the one downshift to fifth, instead taking the entire corner in top gear. The act of downshifting (in my previous technique) had been producing a momentary dose of engine braking, resulting in my final entry speed dropping down to the 95-100 MPH range. The absence of this downshift (in my new approach) resulted in an increased entry speed, closer to 105 MPH. As I got the bike leaned fully over, entering the corner, I sensed that my

33

speed was at the upper limits of traction and was forced to halt the normal throttle roll-on. This was done in an attempt to avoid exceeding the maximum allowable speed, by the time I reached the apex. The lack of applied throttle, naturally, resulted in an excessive percentage of the bike's weight being applied to the smaller front tire (i.e. MASSIVE FRONT-END SLIDE!!!) To say that my eyeballs were bulging would be a major understatement. Fortunately, the sliding front-end scrubbed off enough speed that I was eventually able to get back on the throttle again, just in time to avoid an inevitable visit with Mr. Asphalt. Needless to say, that was the last time I tried sixth gear in that corner on my FZR.

*The lesson to be learned, from this experience, is that it is **MUCH** better to approach a corner at a speed that is a little **too slow**, where you will simply end up applying a bit more throttle than you planned through the exit, than it is to come in **too hot** and have to cease the roll-on (or even roll-off) to control your mid-corner speed.*

* * * *

MAINTAIN A RELAXED GRIP ON
THE HANDLEBARS WHILE CORNERING

It's very hard for most novice riders to accept this concept. Novices typically feel much safer when they maintain a firm hold on the bike at all times. Their approach comes from the belief that if the bike gets loose in the corner they will be able to overpower it's will, and thereby maintain control. Very few corners on the street or on the racetrack are completely smooth and free of irregularities. Motorcycles have an incredible ability to self-correct for variations to the road surface, that are encountered in a corner.

In most cases, the actual rider's job, for going through a corner, is over once the initial counter-steering input has been completed and the bike has achieved the desired lean angle in the turn. At this point, any input that the rider applies to the handlebars (including resistance to the automatic self-correcting effects by the bike to road surface irregularities), will only succeed in producing a negative effect on the bike's handling. The gripping of the bars unconsciously causes the rider's body to form a rigid link, tying the front and rear portions of the motorcycle together. This link prevents the front and rear portions of the bike from reacting independently to the unique surface changes that each one is encountering, at any specific moment in time. The bottom line is this: once you are into a corner, the less input on the handlebars, the better!

One other riding situation, that makes it even more difficult to avoid placing unwanted pressure on the handlebars, is while shifting your body weight off to the side of the motorcycle, while moving into the "hanging-off" position for an upcoming corner. It's a natural reaction to use your arms as a tool to change your body position, but it's a major NO-NO. All support for shifting of the riders weight should be done **with the legs**, on the footpegs. The hands and arms should remain completely relaxed throughout the complete transition from sitting mid-bike in the straightaway, to the complete knee out riding position for the corner. The easiest way to achieve this goal, is to think of the handlebar grip as if it were the shell of an uncooked egg in your hand; one that you wanted to avoid breaking during the execution of the entire body transition process.

* * * *

ACTUAL RIDING EXPERIENCE:

Our "Sunday Morning Ride" group consists of well established riders, who recognize each others ability levels and generally ride well within their limits. Our early morning breakfast run is normally taken at a brisk, but sensible pace. It's a time where everyone is shaking the cobwebs from their riding skills, while using the cool crisp morning air to whisk away the pressures of a hard week at work.

I usually lead the group on this breakfast run, acting as the rabbit, while keeping the pace at what could be described as sane, but still exhilarating. To keep the front pack close enough to maintain a sense of camaraderie, throughout the entire run, I *try to maintain a speed that is challenging, but still within the safe limits of <u>all</u> the front runners. This pace is often slow enough that I personally am riding at around the 60% level. I enjoy this pace, however, as it affords me a chance to really relax my riding posture and experiment with small changes that could improve my overall riding ability.*

During these runs, I often resort to a training exercise that I have found provides a great method of developing the relaxed grip mentality. The exercise consists of riding through sections of consecutive sweeping corners (left/right/left) with only my right hand on the handlebar, while my left hand is resting comfortably on the top of my left thigh. Once into the corner, the inner thigh area of my outside leg (for that direction of turn) is pushed tightly against the side of the gas tank where it helps provide some additional stability to the chassis, while not upsetting the self-correcting characteristics of the bike. The fact that I am holding the handlebars with only one hand makes it impossible to use my arm to support any body weight during the left/right transitions (as the bike would jerk to one side as the bar was unavoidably turned). This forces me to utilize my legs as the sole means of support, for these side to side movements, as I should.

The first few times I used this exercise, the riders that were immediately following me questioned me inquisitively (upon reaching our breakfast destination) as to my reasons for this rather unorthodox riding posture. Once I explained my objective, they would typically voice their surprise in how fast of a pace we were able to maintain throughout the ride, despite this "handicap".

* * * *

NOTE: Properly executed (and with a little practice) a rider can comfortably keep a pace of 75% or greater of their personal limits, while using only their right hand on the bars. This exercise should be reserved **only** for roads that you are familiar with, and are known to be <u>free of major bumps, potholes, or unexpected traffic situations</u>.

RIDE WITH THE INDEX FINGERS, OF BOTH HANDS, POSITIONED OVER THE LEVERS (BRAKE/CLUTCH) AT ALL TIMES

A quick glance at the typical action shot, on the cover of most sportbike magazines, will illustrate an example of a rider using this technique. Initially you may think that the test rider is doing this solely for the purpose of assuming a more aggressive riding posture for the photo; and I guess it's possible that in some cases that analysis may be correct. However, if the test rider's skill level fits into the top 10% of the motorcyclist fraternity (as most of these individuals do), optimizing their high speed control, is more likely the objective for this behavior.

During high speed sportriding, and during the act of evading unforeseen obstacles, the amount of available time for making control inputs to the bike; is very limited. During defensive maneuvers, the difference between a serious accident and a clear escape, can often be measured in intervals of milliseconds.

There are four primary objectives for maintaining the index fingers resting lightly over the levers:

1) To allow for instantaneous locating of the brake and clutch levers, when a critical moment unexpectedly arises

2) To enable simultaneous application of the front brake, while the throttle is being "blipped", to allow for downshifting; during high speed braking maneuvers.

3) To allow for simultaneous application of front brake and throttle, while trail-braking into corners

4) To minimize the possibility of over-application of the front brake, during the initial grab for the lever

I normally utilize a single finger (my index) for doing **all of my braking**, when riding on the street. This includes some very spirited riding, that requires a strong application of the front brakes to scrub off speed. I've found that using a single finger, acts like an automatic restrictor (or governor), reducing the inclination to over-brake during critical moments.

The brakes on most modern sportbikes are extremely powerful, enabling this single finger braking to be used by most riders (with practice). Utilizing this method, over a period of time, will develop the muscles in the rider's arm and eventually enable a stronger pull with less effort and fatigue.

The only time that I find myself using more than one finger (index and middle only in this case), on the front brake, is at the racetrack. My local track (Sears Point) has two very tight (35 MPH) corners that immediately follow long high speed straightaways, where speeds of over 120 MPH are obtained. In these special situations, with fully heated race compound tires, the bike is capable of accepting, and in need of, more braking force than I can apply with only one finger.

Quickly locating (and disengaging) the **clutch**, in emergency situations, can be equally as important as braking. Downshifting the bike to the proper gear, where adequate power is available to accelerate around the obstacle, is often an integral part of a successful evasive action.

Initially, this technique may feel slightly awkward to you; but be patient because with time it'll become as natural as sitting on the seat. Eventually you'll reach a point where you won't feel totally in control of the bike, without doing it.

Remember that your fingers are merely resting lightly on the top surface of the levers, **NOT** applying any actual pulling pressure that would cause the brakes to unconsciously drag (overheating the brake rotors), or the clutch to partially disengage (slip)!

DON'T FOLLOW SLOW MOVING TRAFFIC

Sweeping down a twisting stretch of two-lane mountain road, motorcycle riders often find their progress suddenly restrained by a procession of slow moving vehicles. The difficulty factor in clearing this moving roadblock (legally) has increased as the number of roads divided by solid double-yellow lines grow every year.

In areas with high potential for law enforcement it may be desirable to avoid passing over this enamel barrier, regardless of the visibility ahead. Recently, one of my favorite local riding areas has become subject to a form of enforcement, for double-yellow passing, that is virtually invisible to the rider. The road is now patrolled by aerial surveillance units (single engine aircraft) that report any violations to awaiting ground units. To say that this situation makes one a bit paranoid about passing over the line, is an understatement.

What options are left, if passing over the lines is not a viable alternative?

1) Remain behind the procession, at a snails pace, for an indefinite period of time (suffering great frustration in the process). <u>BAD CHOICE, BUT COMMONLY DONE</u>!

2) Pull over to the shoulder of the road and wait as long as possible, until the next approaching vehicle comes down the road in your direction, before resuming. This will provide you with a clear stretch of open road ahead, to resume your prior "PACE". If you catch the group, as second time, just repeat the procedure to reopen the road to your style of riding. <u>GOOD CHOICE, NO STRESS</u>!

DON'T ALLOW EXTENDED POLICE ESCORTS

Even the best riding areas, have recently found themselves blanketed with increased levels of law enforcement. One of the tactics that police will sometimes utilize, is to fall in behind a rider or group of riders and follow closely behind for a extended period of time (often 10 miles or more). This technique will sometime net the officer the reward of a moving violation, as the paranoid riders succumb by making a minor riding error, due to their nervous state of mind.

What options does the rider(s) have in this situation?

1) Continue down the road on the original planned route, while closely monitoring the speedometer and all traffic signs, for as long as is necessary for the officer to give up the tail. <u>BAD CHOICE, BUT COMMONLY DONE</u>!

NOTE: Option number #2 is based on a situation where the riders have **NOT** previously been seen, by this officer, violating any traffic laws.

2) Pull over to the shoulder of the road (in a safe and legal turn off point, while utilizing all proper signaling), or turn off onto an adjoining side road, and stop. Get off the bikes and take advantage of the time for a little conversation break. The officer's only options, at this point, are to also stop and confront you for what you haven't done (remember you must be innocent of all violations to pull this off), or continue on down the road. In either case the stress factor is removed and "the ball is placed into his court", where you are again in control of your own situation. GOOD CHOICE!

Chapter 4

Braking Techniques

The entire process of learning how to go FAST, when on the throttle, offers little value if not accompanied by the ability to safely and effectively slow the motorcycle back down. Too many unfortunate riders have met with disaster by trying to master the secrets of speed, disproportionately to their development of high speed braking techniques.

Years ago, while at the tender age of 18, I had my first experience with teaching someone else the very basic techniques of motorcycle riding. I certainly wasn't a great motorcycle rider, at that young age, but I was fortunate enough to have the logical sense on how to systematically go about developing skills in an activity that has a high level of risk associated with it. I feel that the method I used at that time (and have used successfully since), to teach this new rider how to develop his braking skills, is still valid for all riders today.

BRAKE TRAINING EXERCISE:

I recommend this training exercise for any rider who finds that their answer is <u>YES</u> to any of the following questions:

1) Have you recently purchased a new motorcycle?

2) Are you <u>UNABLE</u> to stop your bike hard enough, with the **front brake** only, to bring the rear wheel slightly off the ground?

3) Have you recently installed new brakes, front suspension parts, or different types of tires on your bike?

This exercise requires that you first locate a large vacant parking lot, or deserted street, where the ground is very flat and the asphalt surface is smooth and free of debris. Select an area where there aren't any obstacles to restrict your activity. From a standing start, point the motorcycle straight ahead and slowly accelerate the bike until you reach a speed of only about 10 MPH (initially). Once this speed is obtained and you feel yourself comfortably positioned in the center of the bike with your upper body braced against the handlebars; firmly squeeze on the **FRONT BRAKE** only (with the clutch pulled in) to bring the bike rapidly to a complete stop. Repeat these steps; each time applying the front brake a little bit harder, until you are able to stop the bike quick enough to cause the front tire to lightly skid and the rear tire to raise briefly off the pavement at the final stage of the stopping process. WARNING: remember to approach this level gradually, building your skill and confidence until you achieve the desired results (a *"STOPPIE"*).

Once you have mastered this technique at the low speed of 10 MPH, you may gradually increase your approach speed, until you achieve a point where you feel you've reached the limit of your own personal abilities. In successfully completing this exercise, you will have permanently stored into your memory the maximum braking capabilities of you and your motorcycle (under ideal conditions). In the event of a future emergency situation, you won't have to consciously think about your braking limits, as this stored information will automatically be recalled and applied.

If you're a more advanced rider, you may have quickly skimmed through the discussion of this braking drill, as you feel that your braking skills are already equal or beyond this basic level. You may be correct in that assessment, and if so, the basic drill above probably wouldn't really benefit you. However, even for advanced riders, there is a modified version of this exercise that can be applied during the course of a normal Sunday morning ride. This "on the road" exercise can prove most valuable in maximizing the days riding experience, by increasing the rider's level of performance AND control.

* * * *

ACTUAL RIDING EXPERIENCE:

Riding my bike under less than ideal weather and road conditions, has become a tradition for me. The secret for being able to maintain a good pace, under these adverse circumstances, is an extremely keen sense of **traction threshold detection** by the rider. The rider must be able to sample the adhesion properties between the tires and the road surface, dynamically, on a millisecond by millisecond basis. This critical information is derived in <u>very subtle ways</u>. These methods include, minute vibrations sensed through the footpegs and handlebars, detection of (uninitiated) slight lean angle or RPM changes, and general chassis feel.

During the start of any twisty mountain road excursion, I like to do a quick traction sampling, in order to establish a reference point (or baseline) for the level of available grip. I make a special point of insuring that I perform this exercise when riding under any of the following circumstances:

• Roads are obviously wet from current or recent rainfall

• Outside temperature is excessively cold

• Road surface shows signs of debris (gravel, sand, leaves, etc...)

• Asphalt surface questionable due to the road's construction (smooth, rough, grooved, etc...)

To test the available level of traction, I will wait for a clear, straight stretch of road; and while maintaining a reasonably slow speed (20-25 MPH), with the bike in a <u>COMPLETELY VERTICAL POSITION</u>, I will apply enough <u>**front**</u> brake until the front tire just begins to loose traction (skid slightly) and then immediately release the lever.

My brain is registering the amount of force that I was able to apply to the front brake lever, before traction was first lost. This sampling process automatically re-calibrates all the speed programs in my brain for establishing a new <u>maximum</u> safe threshold.

From then on, I can ride at a quick pace (for these conditions) with extreme confidence in the level of control that I have available.

43

If during the course of our ride, I'm alerted, by a momentary loss of control, that the traction conditions have changed; I'll repeat the sampling process on the next available area. This will again re-establish my reference level, for the available traction threshold.

* * * *

Now that we've established a baseline for our general braking skills, let's move on to more specific techniques in their respective riding environments.

PERFORM ALL THE MAJOR BRAKING WHILE THE BIKE IS AS VERTICAL AS POSSIBLE

The amount of braking force that can be applied to the front tire (where 99% of your aggressive braking will be applied), before loosing traction and sliding, is dependent on many factors, several of which I have listed below:

1) The type (softness) of rubber compound used in the tire's construction

2) The amount of actual surface area <u>not</u> used up by the grooves in the tread

3) The overall dimension of the tire (diameter /width/ profile)

4) Traction conditions of the road surface (rain, debris, temperature)

5) Lean angle of the bike during braking

Of these five factors, only one of them (#5) is within the scope of the riders control, once he is on the bike during a ride. We must accept the fact that a particular type of tire, under a specific type of road conditions, has a finite level of adhesion (traction) available. As an example, if we quantify this maximum adhesion level as a number, say **100**, we can illustrate the benefits of vertical braking.

During cornering, the front tire's adhesion properties are already being called upon to withstand the side forces placed upon it by the turn. The amount of side force that the tire must

44

withstand is dependent on many factors (speed, turn radius, etc...) but for our example let's say that we are using up **75%** of the tires adhesion level for cornering (**100 - 75 = 25** remaining). Therefore if we were to attempt to apply even a moderate level of front braking at this time (say a level of **40**), we would be exceeding the traction limit of the tire, resulting in a dangerous slide.

When the motorcycle is still in a vertical position, prior to initiating the actual turning maneuver, the front tire is not being called upon to withstand any significant degree of loading. Therefore, nearly the entire adhesion capability level of the tire (**100**) can be utilized exclusively for braking, greatly increasing the deceleration potential of the bike. In this vertical position, if the traction limits of the front tire <u>are</u> exceeded by the rider, the resultant tire slippage will not change the lean angle or general direction of travel for the motorcycle, hence bike control is maintained.

A special set of circumstances could occur while riding, where you are called upon (by an unexpected obstacle, i.e. another bike crashing, a rock or debris, etc...) to apply a heavy degree of braking, even though you are already well leaned over into the turn. In this situation, believe it or not, you will still want to apply this hard vertical braking rule (perhaps more importantly than ever). In this situation the rider should momentarily straighten the bike as much as possible (via a forceful countersteering input to the bars), then, immediately upon reaching this vertical position, apply maximum required braking to scrub off the necessary speed, and finally re-initiate the proper lean angle (via a second forceful input to the other side of the bars) to steer clear of the obstacle. This may seem like an impossibly complex sequence of actions to perform, in such a short interval, but with practice it IS POSSIBLE!

* * * *

ACTUAL RIDING EXPERIENCE:

It was a clear Sunday afternoon in July, with everything on our ride going as usual. We had acquired a good sized pack of riders and were really enjoying the adventures of the ride. The road we were on was one that our group had ridden hundreds of times before. Out of repetition, each one of the many challenging turns has been stored into our brains, and archived as if on video tape. To start each ride, we simply push the "play" button, and the rest is refreshingly automatic.

On this particular day not all of the corners would, unfortunately, "playback" as originally recorded. I was riding at the front of the group, on a section of the road that offers a continuous supply of sweeping corners. The average speed for this section of road (in the 80 MPH + range), is somewhat higher than I personally prefer . This is due to an excessive number of long straightaways and wide, increasing radius type corners. At one point along this stretch, there is a farmers open-air type vegetable stand. The stand is very remotely located, and doesn't normally create much automobile traffic.

Entering into a medium speed (approx. 70 MPH) right hander, I had no idea what was waiting around the bend. There are a number of low level rolling grass hills that reside very close to the edge of the road; and in this turn obstruct clear vision of what lies at the exit of the corner. I had just passed the apex (with the bike at maximum lean angle) and had reached a position that finally allowed me to see completely through the remaining half of the turn. The sight that greeted me was NOT GOOD! A small car, that had been pulled off on the right dirt shoulder, was pulling back across the right lane in an attempt to head back down the road in the opposite direction.

My initial reaction was that of panic (but fortunately that lasted only a fraction of a second). Quickly realizing that due to the broadside position of the car, I could not avoid it (at my current speed) by using only a simple steering maneuver. I knew, at this point, that I would somehow have to reduce my speed enough first, to allow me the necessary time (distance) to make an adequate directional change to avoid hitting the car. Recognizing that at my current lean angle, there was no possible way I could apply the necessary level of braking, (without instantly crashing); I instinctively (thanks to many, many hours of practice) had the presence of mind to quickly straighten up the bike, using a forceful counter-

steering maneuver (pressing firmly on the LEFT handlebar end).
Immediately upon the bike reaching a near-vertical position I
applied the maximum amount of __FRONT__ braking that the tire
would allow, scrubbing off as much speed as possible.

As this white-knuckle braking was taking place, I was close-
ly monitoring my progression towards the automobile and
mentally accessing the minimum distance away at which I
would have to release the brakes and take my best shot at an
aggressive steering change. Remembering to __GET OFF__ the
brakes, __before__ actually making the steering maneuver, was criti-
cal. Any steering input applied to the bike, while the front tire is
"brake locked" (or nearly locked) will have little or no effect on
the direction of the bike's travel. The tire must be rotating freely
to initiate any actual turning force.

Viewing the scene I had determined that the car had panicked
and gone for their brakes; rather than the other alternative of
pushing the gas hard to try to accelerate out of the situation. Based
upon this, I decided that the only open path available was to aim
for a pass around the front of the car, as no on-coming traffic was
present and turning the bike back into the corner (working against
the centrifugal forces of this right hander) would have been impos-
sible. At the critical moment, I released the front brake lever, gave
another forceful push on the LEFT handlebar, and was able to
steer the bike just inches clear of the front bumper of the car. The
direction of travel for my bike, at this time, was pointing diagonal-
ly towards the shoulder of the opposite side of the road. Now past
the car, my objective became the need to get the bike quickly
turned back to the right where I would keep the tires on the asphalt.
A quick press on the RIGHT handlebar, for steering, started the
bike moving in the right direction. It became apparent that this
action alone would not get the bike turned the necessary amount,
in the available time, to allow the direction of travel to keep the
bike on the road. I made one final action, consisting of a brief
application of rear brake, hard enough to lock the rear tire for just
long enough to bring the back end around until the direction the
bike was facing would allow me to stay on the road. I released the

locked rear brake, just as the bike reached the necessary pivot angle, and applied some throttle to stabilize the poor straining chassis. I had successfully made it through another one!!

This encounter was definitely what I would call a "close call". All the decisions that I made and all the actions that were taken, occurred in fractions of a second. What percentage of these actions were consciously thought out and what percentage were sub-consciously applied, thanks to thousands of hours of combined riding and racing, I really can't say. One thing is for sure ; knowing the proper evasive techniques, and practicing them, under less stressful conditions, will significantly increase your chances when one of these situations arises.

* * * *

REAR WHEEL BRAKING, SHOULD I OR SHOULDN'T I???

Bring a group of ten sportbike riders (or even roadracers) together and ask them this question. The responses you'll get will probably be as varied as the personalities of the riders themselves. (It does provide the makings for some interesting debates, however!).

I have known of some racers that have <u>deliberately</u> disabled their rear brake entirely (by introducing a large quantity of air into the lines) to insure that they weren't tempted to use it in a panic situation. Most racing organizations require an operational front <u>AND</u> rear brake system, however. Many of these individuals are very competent riders, adding support to the *"rear brake should NEVER be used"* fraternity.

To the other extreme; you will find as much, if not more, strong evidence that <u>selective</u> use of the rear brake is instrumental in achieving the ultimate level of riding. If you've followed the recent (during the last two years) ups and downs of Mick Doohan's 500cc World GP motorcycle career, you know that he experienced a serious injury to his lower right leg. The result of this injury, was the inability for him to pivot his ankle sufficiently to operate his rear brake lever. No big deal, right? Wrong. Mick's riding style utilizes the rear brake; not so much for slowing the bike down, but instead for steadying the chassis going into and through the corners. It was so important for him to have use of the rear brake, that his mechanic engineered a <u>hand</u> operated lever, as a substitute!

So should YOU use the rear brake in your riding, or not? That's a question you'll ultimately have to decide for yourself; but hopefully not until after you've at least tried the following technique.

REAR BRAKING TECHNIQUES:

1) <u>PRE-BRAKING FOR CORNERS:</u>

The primary purpose for the application of the rear brake, as previously stated, is to help in stabilizing the chassis of the bike when leading up to and entering a corner.

Reaching the end of a fast straightaway, that leads to a relatively tight right hand corner, the rider will need to reduce his speed considerably. Going immediately from full throttle (near the end of the straight) to maximum front braking (as is customary), will cause the front end of the motorcycle to dive dramatically. This sudden forward motion may cause the forks to fully bottom out, and due to the elevated rear end of the bike, the rear tire may come completely off the ground. In this position, the motorcycle is not very stable or in control.

The rider can greatly improve the resultant position of the motorcycle (during this deceleration maneuver) by <u>initially</u> applying a **<u>LIGHT</u>** amount of pressure on the REAR brake lever just <u>PRIOR</u> to the start of the front braking action. The light application of this initial rear braking will cause the back end of the motorcycle to squat slightly, lowering the overall center of gravity of the bike, while only slightly reducing the overall speed. This way when the front brake <u>is</u> applied, the pivot point for the natural forward motion of the bike will occur at a point closer to the ground; resulting in less front end dive and rear end lift. The rider can then achieve a higher level of overall braking, without putting the bike into an unstable condition.

To prove or disprove this technique, try approaching a familiar corner at a reasonable speed and brake as late and as hard as your skill level will comfortably allow; using only the front brake. Then turn around and repeat the process for the same corner again (at the same speed), this time using the preliminary rear brake application technique. It may take you several attempts to learn the proper point to begin the application, release the lever, and exactly how much pressure to exert.

2) *CHASSIS SETTLING IN ROUGH CORNERS:*

Riding over rough or irregular asphalt surfaces, while leaned over into a corner, can be a very "eye opening" experience for the rider. Keeping the overall chassis of the motorcycle as taut and firmly planted as possible, is the most effective way of negotiating this type of turn. A light application of REAR brake should be initially applied when first entering the corner (even though the throttle is being gradually rolled on) and maintained (dragged) throughout the remainder of the turn. This small amount of resistance applied at the rear of the bike, will result in the rear suspension compressing slightly and thereby keeping additional downforce on the rear tire for traction. This will resist the bouncing effect of the bumps, helping the suspension in keeping the rear tire in contact with the road surface.

* * * *

ACTUAL RIDING EXPERIENCE:

One of my personal favorite backroads, for "sportbike riding", is a road that not everybody I have ever introduced to it, seems to enjoy. The road is approximately 15 miles long and is blanketed with an seemingly endless supply of very tight (and very bumpy) corners. The road is fairly narrow and has no painted lines at all to separate the two directions of traffic flow (so illegal passing is not an issue). The road is extremely isolated, so rarely do we see more than one or two cars (maximum) during the entire stretch. In addition to the tightness and bumpiness, there are numerous camber, radius, and surface traction changes that occur over the course of this ride.

In several sections, the road has dips and rises that occur at very inopportune times (while to bike is severely leaned over at the exit of a corner). One of these dip/rise transitions, in particular, can be particularly difficult as it lies at the exit of a tight uphill lefthand corner; right at the location where the throttle is coming on strong.

Taking this corner exit, using the standard riding technique: throttle on, brakes off, bike leaned over, (as I did the first few times); results in a very adrenalin rushing experience. As the bike crests the rise, with the throttle applied, when the rear tire reaches the top of the hump; the back end of the motorcycle becomes severely unweighted, causing the rear tire to lose grip. The centrifugal force of the cornering loads immediately take advantage of this unweighted condition, causing the back tire to swing outward. The result is a bike that is trying to go sideways up the hill, in a rather unconventional manner.

*The solution to this corner's problem, was find a way to keep more weight down on the rear of the bike at the moment it was climbing up the face of the hump's incline. I found that applying a <u>moderate</u> amount of **REAR** brake, while approaching the obstacle, caused the back end of the motorcycle to compress slightly, increasing the downforce and thereby maintaining better contact and tracking over the surface of the rise. This prevented the rear tire from actually losing traction at any moment, allowing the centrifugal forces to be kept in check.*

Using this technique on any road, where the surface drops away quickly (as when cresting the top of a hill), will result in improved traction and control. The top of the hill in the infamous "CORKSCREW" (at Laguna Seca) is a perfect example of a corner where this technique can benefit the rider.

* * * *

Do these "rear braking techniques" work for everyone? Probably not. Proper application of this tool requires an extremely sensitive touch by the rider. This is definitely a situation where "too much" can be a very bad thing!

Chapter 5

Line Selection

What's a line? A *"LINE"* is nothing more than a specific path of travel covered by the motorcycle, during the execution of a turn. A properly planned and executed turn, will result in the **actual** "LINE" (the path taken by the bike) and the **intended** "LINE" (the one the rider saw in his brain) being identical. The proper corner entry position, speed, throttle control, steering input, and timing, all play major roles in determining the riders success in creating this harmony.

OK, so if taking the right line is important, tell me what is the ideal line for <u>all</u> corners? Unfortunately, there isn't a single "right line" that will work best for <u>all</u> corners, as not all corners are alike. To simplify this issue, and offer a few general guidelines, let's look at the characteristics that make *"THE RIGHT LINE"* for a corner:

"THE RIGHT LINE" TYPICALLY OFFERS ....

1) the <u>straightest</u> possible path through the corner

2) the highest obtainable **exit** speed from the corner

3) optimum use of all camber changes in the corner

The most common mistake novice riders make, in their LINE selection, is TURNING INTO THE CORNER **TOO SOON**! A lack of confidence in their turning skills is usually the primary reason these riders execute this maneuver. They feel that an additional margin of safety can be achieved by turning the motorcycle into the corner nice and <u>early</u>, and hugging a very tight inside entrance line. Having found, from past heart stopping experiences, that the motorcycle often drifts outward, as they navigate their way through corners, they feel that starting the turn early and as close to the inside as possible, will allow them the maximum amount of cushion ("oops" factor) before the bike reaches the outermost edge of the lane. Unfortunately, they are only compounding their problems, with this improper technique, as it will ultimately force them to make an even sharper turning maneuver to avoid running off the edge of the road.

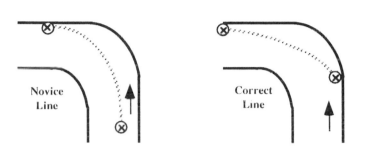

The novice rider's early turn-in technique, is a major violation to one of the "RIGHT LINE" definitions, provided above; as it creates an *effective* turning radius that is even <u>TIGHTER</u> (less straight) than that offered by the original corner. This improper line selection is the first major wall that new riders (unknowingly) run into, when they feel that they're taking a particular corner "as fast as is absolutely possible". The new rider will justify his reaching this limit, by the fact that the bike's tire(s) are actually losing grip (sliding) at this speed. Unfortunately, the <u>overall</u> speed is not the cause of the sliding; it's the speed versus the *resultant* turning radius (being induced by improper line selection) that's creating this symptom. The novice rider is quickly made aware of this fact, when a more experienced rider enters the same corner (in front of him), at a speed 15 MPH faster, and comfortably negotiates the entire turn without incident, before disappearing off into the distance. The novice rider may be left scratching his head, in contemplation of what deficiency in his motorcycle (i.e. bad tires, worn shock, etc...) must be the cause of his inability to take the corner at that same speed.

* * * *

ACTUAL RIDING EXPERIENCE:

Occasionally, I'll end up getting a late exit out of the parking lot, for our Sunday morning breakfast ride, with a resultant "back of the pack" initial riding position within the group. This position ends up offering a refreshingly different perspective on the ride, and is always an educational experience. As a seemingly endless supply of twisting corners fall quickly behind, I find myself methodically working my CB-1 up through the group. Approaching each rider from behind, I pause briefly in my ascent, to allow a moment of up close observation of their riding style. I find that each rider passed, applies their own small variation to the basic line being used by the group. Some riders show a good choice of line selection, and it's reflected in their smooth flowing motion through the esses. Others deviate, in varying degrees, from the optimum line, and it too reveals itself in their rate of progress.

Coming up on the last few riders, who were leading the pack, I expectedly find their line selection to be the best of the group. Observing them, I can only see a few minor variations for improvement. The process of passing these leading riders required that I achieve a specific pace; a pace just slightly faster than the one they were setting, at that point. Surprisingly, I often find that after passing these last few riders, and continuing to maintain the same slightly quicker pace, a member of this lead pack magically remains in close contact, rather than slowly dropping away, as would have been expected.

The first time this happened I assumed the cause was a certain level of competitiveness surfacing, resulting in the riders pushing themselves harder to stay near the front. Being curious by nature, on one Sunday morning after reaching our breakfast stop, I decided to ask the rider who had been immediately following me, as to the reason for his accelerated pace after I had passed him. He replied that by following exactly in my path, the lines he found himself taking allowed a smoother, more controlled execution of his turns. He also commented that he didn't really feel like he was going any faster than before, but the results were obvious (smooth is fast).

TYPES OF CORNERS:

Slipping down a twisty stretch of mountain road, on an early morning ride, offers the rider hundreds of challenging corners. Initially, in looking at these corners in <u>VERY</u> simplistic terms, they can be broken down into <u>only</u> two basic categories; **left** turns and **right** turns. Analyzing the turns a bit more closely, these two main categories can be further classified, based upon their "radius of curvature" (decreasing, constant, increasing). Looking even deeper, other conditions like camber changes (banking of the road) and road surface types, come into view. The entrance and exit characteristics of the corner (corner leading to another corner, or corner exiting onto a straightaway) also play a major role in determining the most advantageous line to be used for that turn. In effect, like every motorcyclist, every turn is unique, possessing a specific set of characteristics that give that corner it's own "personality". Taking the time to learn the "personality" of all of the corners on your favorite road, and how to best approach them, will greatly enhance your overall riding experience.

The examples shown on the following page, illustrate the basic line for each of the three major types of radius corners. Though the actual lines are very different, the objective is the same in all cases; <u>maximize **exit**</u> speed while <u>minimizing</u> the required curvature of the turn. Keep in mind that other factors (camber angle, surface traction, etc...), not represented in these illustrations, may greatly impact the optimum line for each of these corners.

* * * *

ACTUAL RIDING EXPERIENCE:

In preparation for the start of the 1993 roadracing season, at my local track (Sears Point), I purchased a brand new "49-state" version of the Honda CBR-600F2. Moving up from the 450 class to the 600 class would mean racing against some tougher competition. None of my previous top-10 competitors, from the 450 class, had made the same switch, therefore it would be a completely new pack of racers I'd be up against.

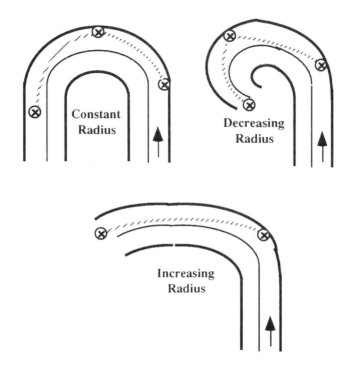

Constant Radius

Decreasing Radius

Increasing Radius

It didn't take too long (the first couple of races) to establish a "pecking order" amongst the pack of 60 or so racers. I found myself running in the top 8-10 positions, from start to finish of each race. In normal race fashion, the total group of 60 riders would gradually string themselves out into many smaller packs, each consisting of between 3-5 riders, as the race progressed. These smaller packs are comprised of rider's with similar equipment and ability levels, hence turning comparable lap times.

In my unofficial "pack" of riders, there were two individuals in particular that presented me with my greatest challenge. Having raced the 600 class in previous years, both riders (who also happened to be best friends) were quite confident and aggressive in their riding styles. They often locked themselves into a private two-man battle, where they weaved and bobbed their way around the racetrack. I found it very difficult to pass them, despite the fact that I was able to go slightly faster through the corners (especially the high speed ones). They both exhibited animalistic braking techniques, at the end of the straights, making it nearly impossible for me to "outbrake" them (though heaven knows how many times I tried; unsuccessfully).

Halfway through the season, I'd only managed to finish in front of these guys on a few isolated occasions (and with many "close calls" as a result). Using input I had gotten from friend's observations, combined with my own brainstorming sessions of the problem, I came up with a calculated "plane of action".

PROBLEM:

The inability I had been having for passing these riders, stemmed primarily from the fact that I was charging up too close to them, on the entrance to the corners. This put me in a position where I was forced to brake when **they** braked, turn into the corner when **they** turned in, and accelerate out at a speed that **they** had selected.

SOLUTION:

I decided that the place to apply my new "plan of action", was Turn 10; a very high speed right-hand corner that leads onto a 110 MPH + straightaway. Leading up to the turn I put myself in a position where my front tire was within a couple of bikelengths of whichever one of these racers I was going to attempt to pass. Slightly before reaching the braking point for the corner, I deliberately backed off the throttle slightly, allowing a calculated gap of about four or five bikelengths to develop between us. Due to this intentionally created gap, I _wasn't_ forced to brake when he did, allowing me the freedom to go deeper into the turn before executing my actual turning maneuver (a later "apex" than he was doing). This late apex would enable me to take the OPTIMUM race line through this corner (one that he was NOT using), resulting in a higher EXIT speed onto the adjoining straightaway. Bringing the bike back up to vertical (from it's lean angle), at the exit, I found myself traveling at a speed 5-10 MPH faster than my competitor. I had to *mentally block out the fact that I was quickly closing on his rear tire (by keeping my visual focal point well past the rider), to enable me the confidence to continue to roll the throttle on <u>hard</u>. Drafting up towards the back of his bike, I waited until the last moment, and then steered my bike slightly to the right (an inside line) of his path. Taking a **<u>too early</u>** apex, he was forced use less throttle and unavoidably drift <u>wide</u> on the exit of the corner, opening up a nice window for me to comfortably slip through while maintaining my higher exit speed. The having been pass made; I would typically reach the end of the adjoining high speed straight with 3-4 bikelengths to spare.*

I would then be able to ride my own race, for the remaining laps, resulting in a pace that would average one or two seconds faster per lap than those done while following these competitors. The remaining races of the 1993 season were a lot more enjoyable, with this new secret weapon added to my arsenal.

* * * *

Chapter 6

Advanced Techniques

"HANGING OFF"

The glossy front covers of most issues of sportbike magazines, are typically graced with textbook examples of this "hanging off" (knee dragging) riding technique. Inside the same issue you may find an article on street riding do's and don'ts, using the riding philosophy and *claimed* behavior of the editorial staff, on their personal rides, as models to follow. The article preaches the importance of following the examples of the editor's non-exhibitionist riding styles, used as they practice the so-called "PACE". In their definition of this style, they discredit the use of any "hanging off" as unacceptable behavior. What about those cover shots, obviously taken on some stretch of public road? A double standard perhaps? I think so.

What's the proper path to pursue then; should we follow the advice given in the text of the article or should we emulate the actions depicted in the pictures? Perhaps we can find an approach that offers a compromise on this issue. Taking just a moment to analyze the pros and cons of this type of riding style, may help in deciding if it's really right for you.

PROS:

• It allows for a lower center of gravity on the bike increasing rider control

• It allows the motorcycle to be leaned over a lesser amount (for the same speed and turning radius corner) increasing ground clearance for metal parts on the bike (pipes, brake levers, etc...)

- The more vertical position of the motorcycle, provides a reserve of available tread surface on the side of the tire, if needed for emergency maneuvers

- The knee puck (assuming the use of full leathers) can be used as a safety valve to help support some of the weight of the bike in the case of an unexpected slide, often allowing the rider to avoid a crash

CONS:
* It attracts attention (mostly UNDESIRABLE) to your riding from law enforcement and the general roadgoing public

- It can actually have a negative effect on your bike control, speed and safety, **if improperly** executed by inexperienced riders (merely in an effort to copy the riding style of their racing heroes)

If you think that the "hanging off" style may be of benefit to you, there are a few important guidelines that should be adhered to. This technique should only be fully applied when the rider is outfitted with a **complete** set of leathers, with knee pucks installed. The current riding environment also plays a big part in making the right decision on whether *to do* or *not to do*. This style should **NOT** be used in highly populated or congested traffic areas, like city streets or on heavily traveled public roads and highways. It should also **NOT** be used for the purpose of "SHOWING OFF". The only *RIGHT* reason for using this style, is the desire to improve your riding ability and control of your motorcycle. The application of this technique should be reserved for those very special stretches of open road, that reside on your own personal Sunday morning ride. These stretches should be clear of excessive automobile traffic, houses, stop signs, and most certainly, law enforcement.

APPLYING THE TECHNIQUE:
The first, and probably biggest, mistake that riders typically make, when first trying to apply this "hanging off" technique, is

using their arms to pull their body weight from one side of the bike to the other. I have known a few riders who swore themselves away from ever using this style (again), after having experienced some rather scary moments during their initial experimentation. The transition of the body's weight, from one side of the bike to the other, **should** be accomplished solely by the use of the **riders legs**. The arms (and hands on the bars) should remain completely relaxed, allowing only for a slight repositioning to the angle of the rider's grip. Improperly executed, the pulling effect on the handlebars will result in an unexpected wobble, as the unintentionally applied dose of countersteering is applied to the front tire.

The second most common error applies to the proper TIMING for the point of initiating the "hanging off" maneuver. Many first time knee draggers think that they should wait until they reach the actual turn in point, at the entrance to the corner, to shift their weight to the inside as the bike is leaned over. They feel that the simultaneous shift of their body weight, at that critical moment, will assist them in getting the bike leaned over more quickly (their quick steering goal is actually an admirable one; one that **is** highly desirable, but not one that should be achieved through body positioning). The proper technique consists of completely FINISHING the transfer of the rider's body to the "hung off" position, **BEFORE** the bike even reaches the actual pivot (lean in) point for the turn. This means that this entire operation should take place near the end of the straightaway, while the bike is still in a completely vertical position.

Now obviously there are circumstances where the rider must negotiate consecutive corners, without any straight section between (S-Turns). In these situations it is more critical than ever, that the rider be extremely SMOOTH in his body transitions, to avoid upsetting the bike. As no straightaway exists in these situations, the transition of weight will have to occur much more quickly. The rider should still attempt to do as much of the actual body weight movement (as possible) in that small window of time when the bike is at or near vertical (during the transition from left to right lean angle).

61

SIMULTANEOUS APPLICATION OF
FRONT BRAKE AND THROTTLE

This technique may at first seem very strange and contradictory to all of the basic rules you've learned since operating your first motorized vehicle. The basic rule has always been that you should **either** be applying the throttle (accelerating) **or** applying the brakes (decelerating); certainly NOT doing both at the same time. At first glance it certainly seems counterproductive to be feeding the bike any throttle at a time when the brakes are being applied; after all if you're using the brakes your objective must be to decrease the speed of the motorcycle. The main objective for the usage of this rather unusual technique, is to attempt to maintain the optimum weight distribution on the bike (60/40) at a time when the normal physics of the action (late braking into a corner) would cause this balance to be severely violated.

My learning and developing of this technique was brought about primarily out of necessity. I pride myself as being a year round type of motorcycle rider and often find that I'm the only sportbike "on the hill" during a steady November downpour. I can certainly understand why the other riders have remained at home on a day like this, but find it personally challenging to be able to maintain a reasonably brisk pace under these adverse conditions. I believe that a rider can learn more about throttle control, braking, traction sensing, and proper lines in a single day like this, than he'll learn from months of dry weather riding, at any speed. The "forgiving factor" that the road offers for rider technique errors, on rainy days, is very narrow; rewarding exactness while unfortunately penalizing even the smallest of mistakes.

In thinking about specific riding conditions where this technique most applies; three different types of situations come to mind.

1) **Downhill, off-cambered corners:**

Approaching a corner of this type will naturally require some initial braking to set up the proper entry speed. However due to the acceleration effects of gravity, once the brakes are totally released and the bike is leaned into the corner, it's speed will automatically begin to increase again. If we adhere to the basic throttle rule, by steadily rolling the gas on throughout the turn, our mid-corner speed will likely exceed the maximum traction limits of the bike's tires. One option then, to prevent this excessive mid-turn speed situation, is to violate the throttle rule by rolling off slightly in the corner, to compensate for the acceleration effects of gravity. The problem with this course of action is overloading the traction limits of the FRONT tire. Gravity has already caused an excessively large percentage (more than 40%) of the bike's weight to be placed on the front tire, and the act of rolling off the throttle (even slightly) will result in even more weight being shifted onto the overloaded contact patch.

The necessary task at hand, is to do the following:

#1: maintain a **constant** safe speed through the entire corner (resisting the acceleration effects of gravity)

#2: prevent an excessive amount of the bike's weight from being transferred onto the **front** tire.

The solution is quite simple; **simultaneous application of throttle and front brake!**

As the bike approaches the initial turn-in point, the front brake is still being utilized. When the bike is leaned into the corner and the throttle is begun to be applied, rather than completely releasing the front brake lever, release it partially while still maintaining a moderate amount of pressure. Slowly roll on the throttle, but only until you can just feel the engine working gently against the slowing forces of the brakes. Continue to maintain a gentle amount of brake pressure throughout the entire length of the turn, gradually releasing it as the bike is eventually straightened up during the exit of the corner. The throttle position **must** be maintained at a constant level where the sound of the engine continuously indicates that it's working lightly against the braking forces. This will insure that the necessary amount of weight is kept off the front tire and transfer it, through the bike's chassis, to the larger rear. The feathering of the front brake, will insure that the mid-corner speed does not reach a point where it will exceed the maximum traction limits of the bike's tires, despite the applied throttle and effects of gravity.

2) Wet weather cornering:

The execution of a turn, in wet weather conditions, requires that the maximum safe speed for available traction <u>not</u> be exceeded at any point through the corner. <u>Entering</u> the corner already at or near the maximum safe speed, when combined with the standard throttle roll-on rule (previously discussed), will result in a mid-corner speed that will be in excess of this limit (if no other steps are taken). The secret to avoid this condition, is the application of the same basic throttle/brake technique, described above, where the gas is smoothly and moderately rolled-on throughout the corner (for weight transfer) **AND** a <u>constant</u> light pressure is maintained on the front brake lever (to prevent any undesired increase in cornering speed).

The application of this technique, will consistently amaze any riding partner with the speed <u>and control</u> that you will be able maintain while negotiating turns in the wet.

3) Contiguous sets of corners (left/right/left, etc...):

Getting through a set five consecutive and varying difficulty corners, in the shortest period of time, is best achieved by being "SMOOTH". Charging into the first or second corner, only to find yourself hard on the brakes to avoid overshooting the third (being a decreasing radius turn), will result in slower overall speeds as well as a potentially dangerous situation.

For this example set of 5 corners, lets say that the first two turns are fairly wide open, allowing a speed of approximately 60 MPH to be maintained from entry to exit. There is a short straight section linking turns 2 and 3 (a 50 MPH decreasing radius corner). Rolling the throttle on, while exiting turn 2 results in a terminal speed of about 70 MPH at the entrance to turn 3. It will obviously be necessary to reduce your entrance speed by 20 MPH (to 50) by the time the bike is leaned into the third corner. There are two different methods of accomplishing this deceleration: the traditional method, and the previously introduced "throttle/brake" method.

Using the traditional method the rider reaches the point (at the end of the short straight) where he is ready to begin his deceleration process. He rolls off the throttle (transferring a lot of weight to the front tire), pulls on the front brake lever (moving more weight up front and compressing the front forks) until his speed has been reduced to the desired 50 MPH level. Once the speed is set, the rider releases the front brake lever (causing the front forks to rise and shifting weight back to the rear) and then applies throttle while entering the corner (shifting more weight rearward, raising the forks an additional amount, and loading up the rear suspension). All this sudden transferring and un-transferring of weight creates a pogo-stick effect and will invariably upset the bike's chassis, causing a lack of stability entering the corner.

Using the throttle/brake method, the rider would reach the end of the straight under the same conditions as above. However with this technique, rather than <u>completely releasing</u> the <u>throttle</u> and then applying the front brake, the rider will **reduce** the throttle but still maintain a moderately accelerating throttle position, while simultaneously applying the necessary amount of front braking to bring the bike's speed down to the desired 50 MPH level. Maintaining the application of some throttle, during braking, will prevent a sudden transfer of weight onto the front of the bike which would upset the suspension and balance. Once this speed has been achieved, the rider will then <u>gradually</u> release the pressure on the front brake lever, as the throttle position is smoothly rolled-on. This transitional process should be similar to letting the clutch out and feeding the gas on, when starting a motorcycle from a complete stop. The subtle braking that is carried into the entrance of the corner, will help prevent an overloading condition on the rear tire and rear suspension, caused by the sudden shift of weight rearward, when the throttle is applied. It will also insure that the front of the bike maintains sufficient load to keep the front forks adequately compressed, optimizing the actual steering head angle for turning into the corner.

Chapter 7

Epilog

The concepts and techniques presented in this book, are not intended to provide all the answers to the challenges that face the modern day motorcyclist. I realize that some of the techniques, that were described herein, may not coincide with those of other very experienced (and accomplished) riders/racers. That fact does not surprise or bother me, for the world of motorcycling itself is not one of "black and white". Each rider must ultimately take responsibility for their own fate; a fate that is primarily based upon personal riding decisions. The contents of this book are merely designed to provide a palette of ideas, from which each rider (reader) can pick and choose those items that fit their own level of riding.

These ideas are derived from the real-life experiences, as viewed through only a single pair of eyes. My personal longevity (20+ years of riding), in being able to continue to enjoy the thrills and excitement of the motorcycle experience, is the best evidence I can offer you, as to their credibility.

I'll close out this section of the book, by wishing you all the best that motorcycling has to offer.

HAPPY RIDING!

Supplement:
Rain Riding
"The Wet Weather Rider's Guidebook"

Chapter 1

Introduction

In many parts of the world, motorcycle riding is a very "seasonal" activity. Minnesota roads, in the middle of a snow packed February day, hardly offer an environment that beckons for a high speed sportbike ride! In these conditions, the undeniable reality quickly sets in, even to the most "die-hard" of riders, that "THE SEASON IS OVER!

The extreme weather patterns that such areas of the country experience, realistically limit a sportbiker's riding activities to a very narrow window that rarely exceeds six months (May - October). This six month riding season is something that these northern sportbikers learn to accept, though NOT willingly! The inability to participate in their favorite activity, for such a long period of time, leads to a form of Mother Nature induced *"BIKER'S FEVER"*.

I consider myself to be very lucky, in this respect, as I've lived in California for the majority of my life. In doing so, the serious inclement weather that these more Northern motorcycle brethren must endure, has never been a limiting factor in my decision on whether or not to ride on a particular Sunday. A *BAD DAY* for me, consists of an outside temperature of 50 degrees F, some heavy rains, and a nasty gust of wind from time to time. Despite the less than pleasant nature of these conditions, they DO NOT provide an obstacle that forcibly restricts riding based strickly upon the laws of physics. The ability to recognize that this time of year does NOT need to become an "off season" for sportbike riding,, is really the basic foundation for this "GUIDEBOOK".

My own personal riding season runs from January to January. That fact alone, is a major contributing factor to the

18,000+ miles that I log each year on my sportbike. This milestone is achieved through weekend riding only, and exclusively on "adrenaline pumping" twisty backroads. No long trips, no commuting, just "canyon carving" at it's finest!

I can't say that my own personal riding behavior (with regard to this extended riding season) is very reflective of the "typical" California sportbiker! I often find myself wondering if I'm the last motorcycle on the face of the Earth, when I complete a 150 mile wet weather riding day, without seeing another solo taillight.

Our local sportbiker's "hangout" (referred to as "ALICES", due it's local restaurant's name), often glimmers from the reflection of well over 100 freshly polished sportbikes on a warm and sunny July afternoon. In sharp contrast, I've often pulled quietly into that same parking lot, on a beautifully clear, but cool, December morning, to find a ghostly vacant scene. I find myself scratching my head in wonder, as the bike pulls to a stop; for the cause of this uninhabited scene.

From many years of observing this behavior, I've come to the conclusion that many California sportbikers have resolved themselves to a full six month moratorium on riding (October - April). Maybe for some, it's an act intended to show some form of for their fellow Northern brothers that CAN'T RIDE. It amazes me that even if the weather surprises everyone by exhibiting "Indian Summer" conditions (70+ degrees and sunshine), but the month is November or December, the number of bikes that can be seen at these normal "stomping grounds", can easily be counted on a single hand!

The degree of enjoyment and personal improvement in my riding skills, that I've reaped from many years of "wet weather" riding on twisty, uncongested backroads; has been immense! I've also had the challenge of taking these skills to their most extreme level, while competing in several "WERA" 6-Hour and 8-Hour endurance roadraces that were held, under near "monsoon" rain conditions.

I've also had the pleasure of observing several other fellow rider's (those who I've finally convinced to participate in this rain riding ritual) dramatic increase in motorcycle handling skills and overall performance, as a result of this form of training. Over the thousands of miles of this challenging form of riding, I've learned many lessons (some the hard way) that have helped allow me to become a safer, more controlled, AND FASTER rider. I feel that much of the personal successes that I've enjoyed in my roadracing career, can be directly attributed to skills that were spawned from riding under these extreme conditions. The high demand for rider sensitivity to feedback from the tire's minute traction signals, and the required level of control to keep a motorcycle tracking in the rain, transcend directly into the world of dry weather riding (especially on a racetrack where the cornering speeds demand regular sliding of the bike's tires).

The desire to produce this "WET WEATHER RIDER'S GUIDEBOOK" has been brought about by my recent realization that very little written material has ever been produced to instruct riders on this subject. An article appeared in a recent edition of one of the flashier British sportbiking magazines, on this subject. I was anxious to read it, as I've typically been very impressed with the "grassroots" level of approach that many of these foreign publications exhibit in their literary format. In reading the article, however, I was a bit disappointed as it failed to effectively address the actual "mechanics" of what a rider needs to specifically do while riding, in order to be successful in these conditions. I thought to myself, "hey I could do a better job than that", and the next thing I knew I was sitting at the keyboard banging away.

I hope that by sharing the knowledge that I've had the opportunity of acquiring from years of "real world experience", in this guidebook, I'll be able to help you in improving your own personal "Wet Weather Riding Skills". I honestly believe that IF you're willing to take the time to read and understand these concepts, and then go out and actually PRACTICE them in the wet, you'll amaze yourself (AND all your *fair weather*" friends) with the dramatic improvement you'll exhibit in your riding skills when the skies clear for the following year's traditional riding season.

Chapter 2

Rain Riding: Should I, or Shouldn't I

Prior to inviting you to embark into the aquatic environment of the "Wet Weather Rider", it would be remiss of me not to provide an objective look at the PROS and CONS that are associated with this activity. Ultimately each rider must evaluate their own priorities, and decide which way the scales tip in the "should I, or shouldn't I" debate.

PROS:

The demands for smoothness, precision, and control, when wet weather riding, provides an ideal arena for honestly measuring a rider's skill level. Rider errors, easily tolerated when the roads are dry, will be met with unforgiving consequences in the rain! Rain riding has the effect of placing a rider's bike handling techniques under a "microscope", highlighting their strengths, while magnifying the weaknesses.

The ideal choice of motorcycle, for this training environment, is one that is light, nimble AND relatively inexpensive. Obviously it may not be practical for all motorcyclists to have the luxury of a spare bike dedicated to use exclusively for this form of "higher risk" riding. However IF it is possible to have a spare bike, it's a good conscious decision to make, especially for a first time rain rider. Personally I lack this luxury, and as such, do my rain rides on the same 1996 GSXR-750 that carries me through the dog days of summer.

In order for a rider to begin to push the envelope of a bike's capabilities, they must be able to develop a precise "feel" for the limits of the tire's traction. Normally (in the dry) the cornering speeds required to fully stress the "sticky" crop of modern sport-bike tires to their traction limits is so great, that it's best left to racetrack outings ONLY. In the wet however, this maximum available traction threshold of the tires can easily be reached without the rider having to take the bike up to "triple digit" speeds. The feel of a sliding tire is very similar, at it's limits, in either of these weather conditions; but the penalties for a mistake at the lower rain speeds, is potentially far less severe to the bike and rider.

Despite the higher degree of precision, that this lack of available traction from the wet asphalt surface demands of the rider, it actually offers an additional "PRO" in form of damage assessment upon the unlikely (we always hope) event of a "get-off". The slippery road surface tends to be much more "forgiving" to the bike's hard parts, as well as to the rider's leathers, gloves, and assorted apparel upon impact.

In observing the trends, in sportbike crashes around the twisty mountain roads of our local riding areas, I've noticed an alarming pattern. In the first few months of the "unofficial" motorcycle riding season, (May, June) we tend to exhibit the highest incident rate of the entire year. I believe that at least some of the blame for this trend, can be attributed to the long "off" period, without any riding, from which many of these unfortunate individuals have recently emerged. It's unrealistic for a rider to expect no degradation in the sharpness of their riding skills, immediately upon returning from six months of having their bike in a "mothball" state. Unfortunately many of these riders are unable (or perhaps unwilling) to recognize this initial "rustiness", and attempt to immediately resume the same pace achieved at the end of the following year's riding season. The "Rain Rider', however, not only retains their old level of sharpness and skill, through these long winter months, but actually emerges from these "days of dampness" with a HIGHER proficiency than the year prior!

CONS:

Unfortunately, as with most things in life, along with all the good "a little rain must fall" (sorry for the play on words; I just couldn't resist). The most common justification that "NON"-Rain Riders have for their decision to abstain, is a higher potential for risk of an incident occurring to them and/or their bike. This is certainly a valid concern, and not one that I will dispute. The slippery traction conditions of a wet road (especially in the early days of a first rainfall), definitely increase the probability for mishap. As previously mentioned, despite the increase in probability, the anticipated severity of the consequences of such an incident, are normally less devastating.

A rider who is new to the experience of rain riding, is understandably more apprehensive about these potential consequences, as their skill level does not afford them an adequate measure of confidence to offset these fears. This situation can be viewed as a "Catch-22" scenario. The rider lacking in wet weather riding skills, is certainly at much greater risk of incident than a seasoned veteran. However, the only way for that rider to develop these skills, is by going out and exposing themselves to many miles of riding under these conditions. The best approach, when seriously entering into this new world of riding, is with a great deal of respect and a reasonable degree of moderation. Start with a few easy rides where the rains have persisted for numerous days, and have had time to wash the roads clear of major road debris (oil drippings, leaves, etc.). You may even want to wait until the actual downpour for the day has subsided, and then go riding on the resultant damp roads, but without the visibility impairment that active rainfall produces for the rider.

The second most common "CON", that "NON" Rain Riders reference, is the increased wear-n-tear that the bike is subjected to when riding in these adverse conditions. Again, a very valid point, and one that I won't dispute. The accelerated wear that the chain and sprockets typically exhibit (despite the most diligent efforts at maintaining proper lubrication) is a side effect of rain riding that must be anticipated. The application of a good water dispersing agent (i.e WD-40), immediately upon returning home from the ride, is the best may to MINIMIZE this impact. I'm able to obtain a full 12,000+ miles from my o-ring style chains, despite the year-round riding to which I my bike is subjected!

The same water and grit that attempts to "do-in" the chain, may also have a tendency to sneak past rubber seals and attack wheel and steering head bearings. Attention to regular maintenance, and the application of a good "waterproof" grease to these areas, will help maximize the life expectancy of these parts.

Besides the mechanical wear issues that rain riding can accelerate, the aesthetic beauty of the bike's "pretty parts" (wheels, lower sections of the bodywork, etc.), will eventually reflect some signs of the harshness of the elements. Proper "pre-ride" and "post-ride" maintenance, to these parts, can also reduce the severity of this wear.

The only magic solution, to totally prevent any signs of increased wear on the bike, is to park it a "mothballed state" during the winter months, and decline to enroll into the "Wet Weather Rider" fraternity. Ultimately it comes down to a personal decision that each rider must make, but hopefully AFTER fairly considering all of the "PROS" and "CONS", and prioritizing them accordingly. Upon performing this sole searching process, IF you're still interested in proceeding into this new world of motorcycling; then turn the page and we'll begin to discuss the mechanics of how it's all done!

Chapter 3

Equipment Requirements

Based on my enthusiasm for the wet weather form of riding, you may get the impression that I'm a glutton for punishment. To set the record straight; let me say that on those few odd occasions where I've gotten caught in a sudden downpour, while still 30 miles from home on my bike and dressed only in my normal clear weather riding gear, I have been MISERABLE! The "FUN" riding that I'm inviting others to explore, are days where I have intentionally embarked upon the ride, knowing well of the impending conditions, BEFORE even leaving my house. The reason that I am able to maintain extreme enthusiasm while rain riding on these days, is because my preparation has outfitted me in riding apparel that allows me to arrive home in a predominantly dry condition, upon having stripped away the protective layers. I'll be the first to admit (from personal experience), that a cold, and soggy sportbike rider is NOT a *"happy camper"*!

There are many forms of claimed "waterproof" riding apparel on the market, and I don't intend to turn this section into a sales platform for marketing of any particular manufacturer's products. However, I will provide some basic guidelines on the "type" of riding equipment, that I've personally found to be most effective in keeping my rain riding experiences in the "FUN ZONE".

In the most severe and longer duration rain riding situations, I've found that only boots, gloves, and a riding suit that are manufactured from a material that COMPLETELY sheds all water (i.e. a rubberized surface coating), will suffice.

RIDING SUIT:

A "one-piece" rainsuit is generally the most beneficial to serious rain riding sessions, as it provides the minimum potential for gaps where water may find it's way in to the rider's clothing. The suit should be purchased in a large enough size that it will fit comfortably over the outside of your normal protective clothing (i.e. leathers with protective armor). The large size is very important so as to not restrict the rider's ability to move smoothly around on the bike during cornering maneuvers.

* * * *

BOOTS:

Few actual leather type boots are TRULY "waterproof", when the conditions become extreme, so I've found the most effective (and coincidentally, least expensive) method of keeping your feet dry, is a set of $20 rubber "outer booties" that can be worn directly over your normal sportbike riding boots. This allows the rider to maintain the same level of "crash protection", while adding in the necessary "waterproofing" to provide for an enjoyable ride, even under the worst weather conditions.

* * * *

GLOVES:

I've yet to find a regular leather style glove that can endure an extended pounding of rain, without soaking through! Therefore the rubber outer type solution (borrowed from the boot issue above) has proven to best "fit the bill", for my wet weather use. Many of the "wet weather" style regular standalone gloves, though offering a higher degree of water "resistance", all offer a lesser degree of actual crash protection to the rider's hands. Many of these thicker "do-all" gloves, also limit the amount of rider feedback that is available through the handlebars of the bike, thereby decreasing the level of control that is afforded the rider in these challenging conditions. By utilizing these rubber outers, over the standard protective gloves that the rider would normally be using, the protection level is not compromised.

These rubber outer gloves should be purchased in a VERY LARGE size, to insure that the circulation in the rider's hands are not restricted, and thereby causing numbness. I've learned that lesson the hard way, when my hands experienced such a high degree of restricted of blood flow, that they ached so severely that I had to bring my ride to an early conclusion. These rubber outer gloves are available at most motorcycle accessory dealers, and normally cost less than $10.

* * * *

STOPPING THE LEAKS:

In order for this waterproofing process to be fully successful, the union between the rainsuit and the gloves, and booties must be scientifically arranged like the shingles on the roof of a house. The water must be forced to travel from waterproof surface to surface, WITHOUT being provided any opportunity to sneak it's way inside. This means that the cuffs of the suit must be pulled OVER the top openings of the gloves AND booties, such that water running down the surface of the suit, will continue on it's path to the ground without any other "paths of less resistance". This step is CRITICAL, or the benefits of the waterproof surfaces of these garments will be lost!

* * * *

HELMET:

Maintaining adequate visibility, when riding in heavy rainfall conditions, can be difficult. The challenging nature of these conditions, demands greater attention than normal, yet attempts to deny the rider that ability through the tendency for "fogging" of the faceshield. Pre-treatment of the rider's faceshield, BEFORE embarking on the ride, is paramount! A clear visor should be fitted (vs. any form of "tinted") and several good coatings of "RAIN-X" (or similar product) should be applied to the outside surface to minimize the amount of "beading" effect that will occur. The benefits of such a coating, are most notable when road conditions allow the speeds to be kept above the 40 MPH range.

The humidity that develops inside the damp warmth of the helmet, will invariably result in a "fogged-up" visor, if precautions are not taken. The application of an "anti-fog" plastic layered liner, or topical "anti-fog" solution spread across the inside of the visor, should be freshly done before the ride. Keeping the visor propped out one detent position, will also help by providing some degree of active airflow across the inside surface of the shield.

* * * *

TIRES:

The selection of tires, for riding in these wet road conditions, is certainly a subject that is highly open to "User Preference". The basic guidelines are to locate a tire with a SOFTER rubber compound (typically a top-of-the-line sportbike tire) that will tend to offer a higher level of overall grip on the much cooler water-laced asphalt surface. The tread pattern and depth is extremely important for disbursement of standing water, that would otherwise result in a "hydroplaning" of the tires. Used tires, that were left on the bike at the conclusion of many fast miles of summer fun, may have offered adequate grip in the dry, but should not be chanced during the subsequent rainy months. The best rule of thumb, in these conditions is: "when in doubt, replace them"!

Optimum tire pressures for use in the rain, is another subject that is often cloaked in controversy, from rider to rider. One argument is that the pressures should be **LOWERED** when riding in the rain, as the tires will not produce a normal amount of heat (from road friction), and by lowering the tire pressure it will increase the tendency for the tire to produce more heat.

Personally, from my own experiences, I've come to believe (and recommend to those that inquire) that **INCREASING** tire pressure slightly, when riding in the wet, works best. My thinking is based upon the fact that due to this lack of normally accumulated heat in the tire (vs. riding in the dry), the tire's pressure during the ride, will NOT increase automatically (the typical 4-6 PSI), as would normally occur when riding at a fast pace on a DRY road. The lack of surface friction, from the wet road, (and the cooling effect of the standing water) will prevent any net increase in temperature from occurring in the tire. Therefore this intentionally reduced tire pressure, will have little impact on the ability for the tires to reach the target "riding pressure". If the ideal "target" pressure for the tire, during the middle of the ride, is approximately 37 PSI, then in order to achieve that target in the wet, where tire pressures only rise 1-2 PSI (vs. the normal 4-6 PSI in the dry) the starting "cold" pressure should be **RAISED** from the standard 32 PSI to a more acceptable level of **35-36 PSI**. For me, this technique has proven to provide for an improved level of overall stability and slide predictability, when riding at the limits of traction in these slippery conditions.

* * * *

SUSPENSION SETTINGS:

Due to the decreased overall speeds and available grip between the tires and the road, the bike's suspension is NOT going to be asked to cope with nearly as much "suspension loading". Therefore to insure adequate compliance to road variations, from these lesser forces, it's best to do a general "**softening**" up of all of the available compression based settings. I would recommend DECREASING (turning "counter-clockwise") the compression damping adjusters slightly, at the front AND back of the bike. The "planted" feeling of the bike can also be improved by REDUCING the amount of "preload" on the forks and rear shock. Rebound damping can probably be left unchanged, but ultimately it ends up being an individual Rider's decision.

Chapter 4

Line Selection

There is a great disparity between the ideal riding line for a specific corner in the rain versus the dry. The aggressive, "go in deep, turn it quick and drive on out" method of corner execution, has no place in the wet weather rider's battery of techniques. The level of grip, required for the successful execution of such a maneuver, is simply NOT available on a rain drenched stretch of mountain road. In the majority of cases with wet weather cornering, the **IDEAL** line, is the one that is most effective at "STRAIGHTENING" out the turn. The objective of this "straightening" process, is **MINIMIZE** the amount of lateral (side) force that is placed upon the bike's tires AT ANY SPECIFIC INSTANT, through the execution of the **ENTIRE** turn.

* * * *

To more clearly understand this concept, let's try to quantify the execution of a single corner. Imagine that there is a specific amount of total force that will need to be expended in order for the bike to execute this corner, at a SPECIFIC speed, from entry to exit. For the sake of simplicity, let's say that this total force can be rated as a value of: **100**. To see how this energy will be dispersed over the duration of the turn, we'll divide the turn into **50** EQUALLY spaced distance units, that we'll refer to as "traction points". The following diagram should help in this visualization.

We will then specify that due to the limited availability of traction, that these wet riding conditions present, that the tire's abso-

CORNERING FORCE DISPERSION DIAGRAM:

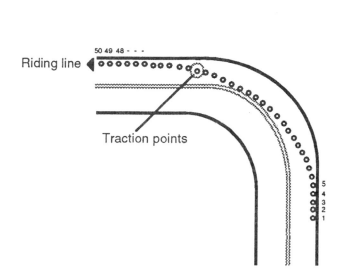

Riding line

Traction points

lute quantifiable limit of grip (at any specific moment) is a force value of "2". With these guidelines established, there is ONLY ONE method to successfully negotiate this turn at the overall desired speed level. That method is to follow this EXACT "straightened out" line of travel through the corner, where you would be applying EXACTLY a unit of force of "2" at the moment that the bike's tires pass across each of the 50 distinct "traction points".

To apply **MORE** energy, than this magic target number, at any "traction point" would result in the tires losing grip, as their maximum traction threshold would have been exceeded.

On the other side of the coin, if the rider were to apply **LESS** force at any of these "traction points", early in the execution of the corner, it would necessitate applying MORE than the maximum allowable force level of "2" at one or more of the subsequent "traction points" further into the turn (assuming the bike has entered at the same initial target speed), to make up the difference. The end result again being the overcoming of the traction limits of the tires.

As you can hopefully appreciate from this example, the demands for **PRECISION** execution of this wet corner (in order to safely negotiate the turn at speed), accept very little margin for error! Granted this is only a theoretical example, but the *real world* conditions of rain riding, are no less demanding.

* * * *

Unlike the racetrack, on public roads proper line selection (for any particular corner) must ultimately take other key factors into consideration. The centermost portion of the lane should be avoided as much as possible; especially while the bike is being subjected to any degree of lean angle. The constant trail of residual oil, transmission fluids and antifreeze from automobiles, always ends up calling this portion of the road it's home. The relatively invisible paths in which the car's tires track, is the safest portion of the lane to travel. The repetitive passes over the surface in these areas, by a multitude of car's tires, will have effectively "vacuumed" this portion of the lane.

On an excessively debris laden wet road, I will sometimes place my tires in one of these car tire paths, at the beginning of the turn, and then track precisely in it's course throughout the entire execution of the corner. I concentrate on looking far ahead, and keep my eyes visually tracing the tire track pathway throughout the execution of the entire turn, in order to simplify the process of holding this exact line. The old adage *"where you look, is where you'll go"* is SO TRUE! Though this may admittedly NOT be the "ideal" line to pursue, based upon the criteria previously mentioned for "straightening" out the corner, but the traction conditions available take priority and dictate an alternate plan.

The one other wet road obstacle that demands a religious application of avoidance technique, are "PAINTED" lines! To quantify the importance of this consideration, if we were to say that there was an available traction level of "6" (on a scale of 1-

10) on the clear sections of wet asphalt, you'd be lucky to find anything more than a "2" waiting for you as your tires pass across any of these painted surfaces!

There are not *cast in concrete* rules for line selection, in the world of rain riding on public roads. It ultimately becomes the skilled wet weather rider's responsibility to maintain his visual focal point far enough ahead, to be able to make the necessary adjustments **BEFORE** committing to a specific line for a corner.

Chapter 5

General Rain Riding Techniques

"SMOOTHNESS" is the common bond that is shared in the riding styles of all proven proficient "Wet Weather Riders". To watch a highly skilled rain rider in action, is to observe a two-wheeled ballet of fluid motion. No sudden braking, no abrupt steering inputs, no aggressive throttle application; just a series of contiguous and minute actions, performed in a well choreographed from! The skilled rain rider is the one who typically, at first glance, appears to be going SLOW. The extreme degree of SMOOTHNESS exhibited, masks the deceptively fast speeds that are in reality being achieved.

* * * *

STEERING:

"COUNTERSTEERING"; anyone who's done any reading on the techniques of performance motorcycling has been inundated by this term. The old *"turn LEFT, to go RIGHT"* concept, is an integral part of any competent rider's repertoire of techniques. Believe it or not, my recommendations on the method of effectively steering a motorcycle, on damp and slippery roads, is going to contradict all those years of training!

In order for the physics of "countersteering" to be applied effectively, there must be a minimum amount of available grip between the road surface and the tires. In order for the lateral force, that is applied to the off-center portion of the tire's tread area, when a "countersteering" action is initiated, there must be enough adhesion to cause the tire to push the

84

bike upright which ultimately results in the reverse turning direction of the front wheel. Though this required level of grip is always present on sticky mid-summer days at the race-track, the world that the "Wet Weather Rider" inhabits, lacks such advantages!

The steering methods used by the highly skilled "rain rider", has closer roots to those early days (as a child) when riding in one of those treacherous "LITTLE RED WAGONS". In these dangerous contraptions, you steered *"left to go left, and right to go right"*. If you didn't shift your body weight to the inside, while making a tight turn, the result was usually the ominous "**HIGHSIDE**". Few of us EX-Little Red Wagon jockeys, can deny having had a least one of these rather heart-stopping experiences.

During wet weather riding, in order to successfully apply this desired *"turn LEFT, to go LEFT"* technique, it becomes necessary to counter-balance the bike's weight as much as possible to the inside of the corner. This is accomplished by using the rider's body as an "OUTRIGGER" (or "IN-rigger" in this case) device, to allow the bike to remain as VERTICAL as possible, despite the fact that it is in the process of negotiating a turn. It is **ESSENTIAL** that the bike be kept in this "near vertical" attitude, for this *"turn in the direction you wish to go"* technique to perform properly. Failing to maintain this position of the bike, will effectively neutralize the ability to use this form of steering technique!

This riding position ("hanging" off the inside of the bike, to some degree), is really not all that unusual of an act, as a road-racer at track speeds, is doing the same thing to maximize the bike's ground clearance in a turn. The only difference when applying this body position during rain riding, is that the amount of "hanging off" may appear (to the untrained observer) to be excessively great for the actual numerical cornering speeds that are being obtained. The major benefit, that this "vertical as possible" bike position provides for the "Wet Weather Rider", is that if/when the bike's tires lose grip at any point in the corner, the bike will move laterally towards the outside of the turn, but the LEAN ANGLE (and resultant level of control of the motorcycle) is NOT adversely effected.

If a "leaned over" motorcycle's tires were to lose grip (of which they surely will) for as little of a LATERAL distance of 6 inches, the resultant increase in the bike's lean angle would most likely put the rider quickly onto the pavement! I've experienced situations, when riding in the rain, where the bike's tires lost grip in the middle of a corner, and the subsequent slide took the bike LATERALLY across the majority of the full 8 feet of lane, before eventually finding adequate grip to halt the process. Despite the initial "heart pumping" reaction, the bike remained in control throughout the ordeal, and was still upright at the conclusion of the turn. Certainly not a maneuver that I'd take to this extreme DELIBERATELY, but one that was ultimately controllable, nonetheless.

* * * *

The sensation of steering a motorcycle in this manner, while hanging a significant distance off to the inside of the bike, can be compared to that of steering an automobile while sitting in the PASSENGER'S seat (as many of us may have done as children, with our parents supervision). This is NOT a technique that comes "NATURAL". In fact, it will require that the rider overcome the deeply imbedded instincts, that many years of "countersteering", have impressed into their brain. Basically the "Wet Weather Rider" needs to have two distinctively different motorcycle handling routines "PROGRAMED" into their brain, one for wet and one for dry; with the ability to switch instantly when the rains begin to fall.

Start SLOWLY, when attempting to begin to apply this form of steering technique. Get a feel for how the motorcycle reacts to these type of inputs, and the importance of the inside body shifting to make it work successfully. This rider's actual shifting of body position, should be completed **BEFORE** actually reaching the "turn in point" for the corner! This "PRE-positioning", will allow for the upsetting effect on the bike's chassis, from all of these rider body movements, to have dissipated. This aspect of the "inside body positioning" technique, is CRITICALLY IMPORTANT!

* * * *

THROTTLE CONTROL:

Having the bike's tire(s) lose traction, and slide at some point in a wet corner, is quite common. As unnerving as this sensation may initially be for the *Novice* rain rider; experienced wet weather pilots learn to be very comfortable with this event. In fact, the most serious of rain riders (myself being one of them), actually get some degree of "adrenaline rush" from each of these occurrences! This natural "high", is one of the incentives that makes all the equipment preparation, mental concentration, and additional level of risk, seem worthwhile!

The occasional slipping of the bike's tires, when riding in the rain, is relatively unavoidable (except those traveling only at a conservative "snails pace"). However, the choice of **WHICH** of the bike's tires (front or rear) is most inclined to exhibit this behavior, **IS RIDER CONTROLLABLE!** The position of the rider's right wrist (the throttle hand), as the bike enters a slippery corner, will directly determine what percentage of the bike's overall weight is distributed on each of it's tires (front vs. rear). As that a sliding REAR tire is exponentially more controllable than a pushing front; the rider needs to insure that they are actually **APPLYING** throttle, by the moment that the bike FIRST begins to enter the corner! The application of throttle, is an effective "weight jacking" device, that can change the weight distribution (front to rear) by several hundred pounds, with only a minute rotation of the rider's right wrist.

In order to insure that the rider has the capability to actually be **APPLYING** throttle, as they enter a turn, WITHOUT accelerating to a speed that would exceed the maximum traction capabilities for conditions; it's important that all braking be completed a sufficient distance BEFORE reaching the corner. The ideal amount of braking, will have successfully slowed the motorcycle down to a speed slightly **BELOW** the maximum entrance speed desired for the turn. This will allow for this CRITICAL application of throttle, to begin at the very entrance to the turn, and continue throughout. The old adage *"when in doubt, gas it"*, holds some serious truths when it comes to safely negotiating a slippery corner. It's FAR better, to approach the corner slightly **SLOWER** than what you had intended, than to underestimate your entrance speed and end up either "chopping" the throttle; or heaven forbid, grabbing a handful of front brake.........AARRGGHH!

Chapter 6

Braking Techniques

BRAKING TECHNIQUES AND
THE "FRONT VS. REAR" CONTROVERSY:

A discussion amongst serious sportbike riders, on the subject of IF and/or HOW MUCH **REAR** braking should be used on a motorcycle, is one that is always be met with heated debate. There's a wide variety of variables that must be considered, when determining one's position on this issue. The riding conditions (wet vs. dry) will play a MAJOR role in the ultimate decision. I'll shed some light on that concept, below.

The amount of available traction, at the back wheel, is the MAJOR deciding factor in whether use of the REAR brake serves any useful purpose. In the maximum traction conditions that are afforded a racer on a sticky set of "slicks" at the track, the amount of weight remaining (i.e. traction) on the rear wheel, at the moment of MAXIMUM braking, is minimal (if existent at all, as the rear wheel may actually raise off the ground!). However with the limited traction that wet weather riding on the street provides, the amount of weight transfer that occurs to the front wheel, is rarely this extreme. Therefore the rear brake can (with practice) be called upon to provide a reasonable percentage (probably around 25%) of the bike's overall slowly capability.

The front brake should still be relied upon to do the "lion's share" of the braking effect, but not relinquished to do the job alone.

The timing of WHEN to actually perform the majority of the braking process, is also extremely CRITICAL! The most effective, and safest technique, is to try to concentrate on doing ALL of the major braking while the motorcycle is as **VERTICAL** as possible! This will insure that the tires are not being asked to devote any of their available traction to absorb cornering forces, and can therefore be fully utilized for the process of slowing the motorcycle down from speed. If the motorcycle is leaned over (even slightly), as when beginning to enter the corner, the percentage of the tire's overall traction threshold that is remaining for the purpose of braking, will have been significantly reduced.

On DOWNHILL turns, where the effects of gravity may tend to cause the motorcycle's speed to increase beyond the maximum desired level for the corner, a bit of **LIGHT** "trailing" of the front and rear brake can be used. This will allow the rider to continue to maintain the smooth, steady and light application of throttle through the corner (necessary to maintain the optimum rear vs. front weight bias, that I previously described), WITHOUT actually increasing the physical cornering speed at which the bike is traveling. This is a technique that should be approached **CAUTIOUSLY,** as the amount of traction that the tires have to spare, for the purpose of braking (when being inundated with lateral cornering forces), is minimal (but **IS** present).

Chapter 7

Epilog

The information, that I've provided herein, is by no means a *MAGIC* answer to all of the issues facing the "Wet Weather Rider". The single most effective method for improving one's skills, for this form of riding, is PRACTICE, PRACTICE, PRACTICE! My own personal abilities, for safely negotiating the slippery conditions of a rain drenched mountain road, came predominantly through this means.

If each rider can find a few concepts in this "WET WEATHER RIDER'S GUIDEBOOK", that they can understand, and eventually apply to their own personal wet weather riding sessions; I will feel that I've been successful in accomplishing my goal.

HAPPY RIDING!